You Drink,
I Die...

Daniel E. Meier

Author Photo by Michael Weber

ISBN 978-1-4116-8720-2

Dedications...

Andrea: for all that is good in my life begins with her.

Dr. Joseph Messina and Dr. Victoria Korth: for your patience and compassion.

Contents _____

Introduction

This work is intended for those of us who grew up with an alcoholic and for those of us who love someone who grew up with an alcoholic. It is commonly reported that one in three people has an alcoholic in their immediate family; father, mother, sister, or brother. I lived with three different alcoholics: father, mother, and brother. This book primarily focuses on my relationship with my father as his disease profoundly impacted my life. It is not meant to judge or condemn anyone. Rather I hope the reader sees it for what it is-one man's journey. It is also intended to open paths of

I

communication among victims of alcoholism. My deepest wish is that at least one of these stories will give the reader comfort in knowing many of us understand their pain.

Living with an alcoholic is like having an elephant in the room, and someone has swept it under the rug. A huge lump exists in the middle of the room, yet no one in the family seems to acknowledge it. Everyone else (outside the family) notices it right away, and is taken aback. Yet, the family living there denies it exists, decorates it, avoids it, pretends it really is not a very big elephant after all, or they stop sitting in the room entirely. The idea of removing the elephant or getting help never occurs to them. My father's alcoholism became the elephant in our house. It took many years for me to recognize my father as an alcoholic, and many more years to forgive him for it. One of the reasons I write this book is in the hope I can learn to forgive myself.

I must forgive myself for many things: for cowering in fear, for numbing out my emotions, for reacting in anger, for believing everyone who loved me would abandon me, for using alcohol to feel normal, for not telling people how much I cared about them, for not protecting myself, and most of all for not loving myself. All of us who live with or have lived with that monster called "alcoholism" must learn to love ourselves enough to forgive ourselves.

By sharing my struggle the reader may see themselves more clearly, gain insight, and learn to forgive the alcoholic in their life, and more importantly forgive themselves. I believe telling my story helped me to forgive myself. Now I give my story to you hoping you will receive comfort in knowing others have felt your pain, and have thrived. My goal is hope.

This story is presented in little vignettes of single incidences. Each is meant to take the reader into the emotions and mind-sets of those involved. Much of my intent is to help the reader truly understand what it feels like to be victimized by alcoholism. Ideally this new understanding will generate empathy, insight, and conversation.

I do not delude myself into thinking this writing will heal the victims. Their wounds are too deep. Rather it may give them voice to seek out help from family, friends, other victims, as well as trained professionals. Healing cannot happen in isolation. The victims need to understand we are not alone, and we need to learn to ask for help. If this book does merely that... I will have done a good thing.

Last Call

The telephone rang around midnight as I lay sleeping. My father was dying. I had taken many calls like this before-my father seemed to be perpetually dying. This would be the last such call I ever received. He had been cloaked in death for so long the idea seemed dull and weak. I almost followed my wife's urging and just went back to sleep. *He would likely pull through again.* Dad had made so many *crisis* calls over my lifetime; I had become jaded and numb to his suffering.

I knew I was supposed to go to his side with my brothers and sisters. Yet, I was tired of this death game he played for so long. The death rattle dance had become an integral part of his manipulations. Part of me wanted to show my contempt by waiting until early the next day. *Rush to his side or go in the morning?* Either choice would have been manlier than the pathetic choice to just dawdle my way to the hospital.

Slowly, I made the one-hour ride to Buffalo in the darkest part of the night. Some complex Jazz from a Toronto radio station kept me intellectually focused and emotionally distracted. Upon arriving at Sisters of Mercy Hospital I sat in the emergency room lounge waiting for events to find me. *I was here, and had done what was expected.* I was minimally committed to being there. Within a few minutes, my oldest brother Marty burst out of the double doors-he seemed odd. It was almost as if he were ready for a friendly conversation… *"How 'bout those Yanks?"* Marty caught himself and ushered me into the emergency wing.

"He's gone. Do you want to see him?"

My middle brother Ted came out and asked why I took so long. I lied and said I did my best. He knew I lied but did not challenge me. Missy the younger of my two sisters, rushed over, gave me a hug, and provided all the technical information: precipitating events, time of death, blah, blah. Missy had replaced my mother as the caretaker of the family after Mom had passed seven years previously.

Dad had been dying for as long as I could remember. As a result, I had mentally rehearsed this moment many times. I was surprised how young he looked without the oxygen hose wrapped around his face. It had been attached to him for years. Without it he seemed more alive (dead) than he had in a long time. I told him I loved him, and on some level I guess I did.

My father was not a good man. I would love to quantify it, but I cannot. This *truth* is all that makes me feel some control over the past. Now that I have complete power over my father, I can say the truth. I am not quite the coward I may seem-telling the truth only after his death. Dad heard the truth from me for a time before he died. He lied, denied, and assured me if he had any memory of it he would be truly sorry: a clever way to conditionally ask for forgiveness. Politicians call that "plausible deniability." I call it lying. It felt good to speak the truth whether he listened or not.

What my father said or did no longer seemed important to me. He had said and done enough-I was full. The rest just flowed over the top of me and dripped down the sides. I was engorged with pain and shame. How had he done this to me, how had I let him, and would it ever go away? Was I strong enough to understand, and move on?

One of the most bizarre parts of growing up with an alcoholic parent is the conflicted memories. Even joyful moments have darkness attached to them. Wherever I am, alcohol is there too, and it infects every part of my life. Joy and darkness are all mixed in together. They are as difficult to unravel as a knot pulled too tight. You can never touch joy without touching sadness. This is why so many of us, who lived with alcoholism, crave sedation. True unrestrained, unapologetic, screeching, giggling happiness does not exist for us. We carry darkness close to us.

I knew my father's passing would not alleviate my pain. It might transform my pain but it would never fade away. I did not anticipate how the stillness, created by his death, would revive so many hidden memories. These memories lurked just below consciousness, as a storm below the horizon gathering strength.

I eulogized my father as both sad and funny. Everyone deserves a kind farewell. I described Dad as a flawed man who likely did the best he could. It has been my experience when people are eulogizing other people they are often

4

subconsciously eulogizing themselves. After all, we understand people based on our own perceptions, and experiences. Similarly, I am also a flawed man who is doing the best I can.

For as long as I can recall, my "best" felt intense, bizarre, and mostly confused. I am the product of an alcoholic father, and an alcoholic mother. Additionally, I am the brother of an alcoholic. Consequently, I have/am suffering from post-traumatic stress syndrome (PTSD), obsessive-compulsive disorder (OCD), and underlying bi-polar.

Thanks to the love of my wife and through psychoanalysis, starting at age forty, I was able see through my illnesses to the pain. My story is the story of millions of people who walk through life in pain and misery resenting goodness and spontaneity, shunning affection, ridiculing less serious people, bragging, lying, and pretending we are doing just fine.

Yet, we are some of the neediest people you will ever meet. I need to tell my story, to let go of my story, to release the power it has over my life, and to let others know that they are not alone. Who is to blame for all the suffering described in this book? I am to blame for not forgiving myself for my own role in my own mental illness. I am to blame, for I continue to let the energy of these events interfere with my own serenity. Maybe by writing it down I can finally let it all go, and be at peace.

Stirred

When I was a child, my father was rarely home. For a while, I thought he worked late. As I grew up, I realized he stopped after work to drink. If he arrived home before I went to sleep I witnessed an ugly, violent scene between him and my mother. At about the age of 10, I started to listen for his car, to scoot off to bed before he got in the house. After a while, I learned to recognize the sound of his car as it turned onto our street about a half-mile away. This was the first manifestation of my obsessive-compulsive disorder as I became hyper-sensitive to my surrounding, and hyper vigilant in protecting myself.

My father was a stranger to me and I was afraid of him, and I wished he would never come home. When he had dinner with us, we children sat in deafening silence. Dad sat at the end of the table drunk, grunting and gurgling, trying not to vomit. On occasion, he ran off to the bathroom to wretch. As we often did, we acted as though nothing happened. Many nights when Dad ate dinner with us, dreadful arguments ensued between him and mother. Eventually one of my parents would involve one of us (children) in their argument. We learned to eat fast and go to our rooms. In general, we could not wait to be anywhere other than home. So we ate fast, and disappeared quickly to our rooms or out with friends.

During my childhood, we rented two different flats. Each was what is called an "up and down:" where one family rents the upper and one family the lower. Therefore, we shared the basement as well as the backyard with the other renting family. In order to escape some of the chaos in our flat, each of us three boys carved out a small piece of the basement to call our own. My father never went into the basement. We did chores like laundry and repairs in the basement, and he believed chores were for women and children. Our basement became a sanctuary for each of us where many evenings were spent alone bunkered in our private basement cubbyholes. My two brothers often shared one large room for building racetracks and model cars. I usually kept to myself by reorganizing part of a storage room, listening to the Buffalo Braves' face the rest of the NBA on the radio, reading books, or sorting baseball cards. I pretended I was the dad and I had a son. I would explain basketball to him, and share some of my best cards with him. Later, I might go out in the driveway and shoot a few hoops with him. Fantasy was often my best companion.

My sisters seemed to always be out with boys. Dating helped them to escape from the insanity. If they were clever, they went out before dad got home. They would meet their friends and dates out somewhere, rather than risk a scene if they were picked up at home. Each of us learned to be careful not to let anyone in to our house for fear that dad would wake up (from sleeping a drunk off) or arrive home drunk and angry.

Mom noticed we always went to other kids' homes, and would wonder aloud "Why don't you ever bring your friends over here to play?" I never answered, just acted as though I had not heard her. How could she ask?

My oldest brother Marty either went out to play baseball in the neighborhood or found somewhere to hide at home. Later in life, Marty tried to be a peacemaker between my parents, but it never worked. However, his attempts at peacemaking usually allowed me to slip away unnoticed, so it did help me a little. When Marty got together with friends to play sports, he would occasionally allow Ted to go along. Ted would end up playing sports against kids three or four years older than he was. He was better than most of the older kids, so they were especially tough on him. Consequently, Ted became a ferocious athlete, and became an all-county high school football player. He was known for his tenacious play.

On a few occasions, Ted ran away (from home) for a few hours. I always thought it was terrific he tried. I rooted for him to make it, and fantasized where I would go if I ever had the courage to run. I even had a notebook of places I might go to if I ever had the "guts." Secretly I hoped somebody would find my notebook and realize how angry I was, and make my home the kind of home I never wanted to run away from. No one ever found it.

Ted's running away would give the rest of us kids a little break. My parents would spend the next few days focused on Ted. Dad would sit at the kitchen table, smoke cigarettes, and make a checklist of potential punishments. Every once in a while he would call Ted to the table to try a few guilt trips on him, without much impact. Ted was too smart or too angry to sit quietly and listen to it-this usually ended up in another argument. Other times, Dad would just come home so drunk; he could not deal with the issue. Mom would ask Ted "How could you do this to me?" and then lament to the rest of us about "poor Ted." Neither parent ever came close to dealing with the issue. Our family was incapable of ever solving problems. Our dysfunctional family attempted to solve problems by worrying them to death.

Ted spent many years in varieties of trouble, even serving a brief prison term for drunk driving. My brother was always angry, and he used alcohol to change the way he felt. Consequently, Ted became an alcoholic. When he drank, his anger became an uncontrollable rage. The fights, fits, and arguments Ted engaged in gave him an overwhelming sense of guilt and self-loathing when sober. These feelings merely fueled his desire for more alcohol. I have read being an alcoholic is like having your hair catch fire, running into the ocean to put it out, and drowning. In other words, the cure for your pain (alcohol) is worse than the pain itself. This describes my brother Ted. The cure (drinking) for his anger and sadness only created more anger or sadness.

After years of alcoholism and drug use, Ted committed himself to a mental health facility. He did so in an attempt to gain favor with a judge who was certainly going to sentence him to prison time for driving while intoxicated. Favor was not granted, and Ted served almost one year in prison. Somehow, at the age of forty he found the courage to reclaim the rest of his life. Ted is married to a wonderful woman and is clean and sober. They share love and much laughter. It is never too late for an alcoholic to change and to establish loving relationships. In many ways, he is and has always been my hero.

My family became something to endure, rather than enjoyed. Rarely was I natural or carefree around my family. Instead, I learned to be guarded with each of them. Each of them has memories attached to them which touch the fear and loathing of my adult-child. I have always felt like an alien abducted by an earth family living in a bizarre scenario trying to pass myself off as one of them. I was the youngest so they shared (between them) many experiences I never had.

I never knew some of the more traumatic events they had suffered. I also never knew some of the better times they shared before the pain permanently poisoned our family. I think they were trying to protect me. Instead, I grew up with an incredible sense of alienation from all of them. I spent so many years living with three alcoholics I had mastered suffering alone. I don't need anyone else's sympathy or understanding.

To this day when I try to discuss a childhood hardship with my siblings, typically they remind me things were worse for them when they were little. You should have seen them back then… providing few details. They intend to help me feel better by knowing I could have had it a lot worse than I did, but I am left feeling as though my experiences are less important. It seems as though if I did not have it as bad as they did, then I have no right to be in pain. My siblings and I should have helped, and supported each other; instead, we belittled each other's experiences, and closed off our feelings. We learned at an early age to keep our pain close, and not to trust or share our pain with anyone, including each other. The only pain our family acknowledged was my father's pain. His pain always demanded everyone's constant attention.

My father was the weakest man I have ever known. He worked as a milkman, and later as a lower level manager of other milkmen. I believed he worked hard and was a very good milkman. As a manager, he was completely overwhelmed. My father knew this new position was beyond his capabilities and felt completely inadequate around everyone he worked with. He medicated these feelings by stopping at a bar on the way home each night. During this time, my father came home late and drunk every night. I went for weeks seeing him only in the middle of the night or on Sunday afternoon.

One of his primary work responsibilities was to make sure that he had a driver for every route. This was only a problem when one of the men "called in sick." The call would come to our home, typically Dad was out drinking, and did not receive the telephone call. Rather, one of us kids would take a message. After he arrived home (typically around 11pm) he started an intoxicated interrogation of whoever had taken the message, often rousting them out of bed. He demanded impossible details concerning the telephone conversation: "When did they call? How did they sound? Did they seem sick? Would they be out the following day also?" Next, he would call the man back in an accusatory tone, and scream at him for calling in sick. Somewhere late into the evening began the process of trying to get another driver to come in on his off day to cover the route. If they refused, he would cuss and slam the telephone down. The entire house had to be in an uproar because he had a problem to solve. All problems became much worse by his intoxicated state.

An alcoholic is the most selfish person you will ever encounter. They are the center of their own sick universe. They are in incredible pain and are completely incapable of shouldering it. What's worse is they want everyone around them to be in pain as well-thereby eliciting some sort of sick kinship. I believe they have a need to see pain in others to let them share the experience. It is as if they are drowning, and they pull the rescuer under as they both drown.

Alcohol temporarily numbs suffering but in the process, creates new shame. Consequently the alcoholic is either numb or in increasingly unbearable pain. They have little knowledge of normal feelings so they must surround themselves with people who can help them support their addiction. To the alcoholic, people who will not support their addiction or disloyal or seem to just want to see them in pain.

We, who live with, and try to love an alcoholic, know the depths of their selfishness. The alcoholic will only let us in to their lives if we play our repetitive roles in support of their addiction. We must care for the alcoholic, provide them with esteem through our successes, entertain them, provide an outlet for their anger, give them excuses to continue their drinking, protect the addiction through denial, disappear to make it easier for them to remain drunk, or we can join them drinking-helping them feel temporarily normal. In fact, the times we seemed most like a family was on holidays, when we all drank together. Regardless of the part we play, we support their addiction and mental illness.

Why do we do this? Survival. Suppose you were in the middle of a transatlantic flight and the pilot came across the speaker and sounded extremely intoxicated. You cannot leave, and you cannot fly the plane. What would you do? You would try to help the pilot stay alert, get as sober as possible, be encouraging, or possibly deny that he was "really" drunk. Maybe he just talks funny. You might radio for help, but what can they really do? They cannot fly the plane for you. You would try everything you could do to survive the flight. My family had a drunken pilot, and a drunken co-pilot, and we all learned to survive as best we could.

We, who live with and love an alcoholic, are sick ourselves. Children cannot pick their parents, but as we become adults, we often choose to remain attached to the disease. Many of us marry alcoholics or emotional cripples. In some way, we are fulfilled through the alcoholic. This disease becomes the only thing that matters in our lives, and without it "Who are we?"

As we pick relationship partners we must ask ourselves...Do I have a need to rescue them? Am I threatened by someone of equal status-thus I must love a pathetic alcoholic? Do they make me feel superior? Do I need to be in control? Do I enjoy other peoples' sympathy? Does being with an alcoholic give me an excuse to flounder-lets me off the hook? Are they dangerous, yet exciting to me? Does their bizarre behavior make me feel normal? Do I believe I deserve to be in pain? These are challenging questions, and most people need professional help to fully develop the answers. I needed professional help, and did it for my family as much as for myself. We must answer these questions for ourselves because the alcoholic is and will always be beyond our control.

I had to love myself enough to ask for help. I had to believe I deserved to feel good, and my wife deserved a healed husband and my children a complete father. Through my own anger, the help of a psychiatrist and through the power of Jesus Christ I was able to put all of us in a safe and loving place.

No Kids Allowed

Most people begin life as children and grow into adulthood. For those of us who begin life in an alcoholic household we tend to live as adults long before our chronological age, and only later do we grow into childhood. I was old long before my time, as Bob Dylan sang… "I'm younger than that now." Other people become adults while victims of alcoholics need to learn to become children.

As a child I enjoyed few carefree moments, displayed little giddiness, and rarely showed any emotion. In my

19

home, the children exhibited complete restraint. We learned not to disturb our parents lest we hear the scream "Knock it off!" This may not seem so different from many homes except while we were expected to be completely mute, our parents were terrifically out of control. We children became the calming influences, the rational problem-solvers, and the peacemakers. We became the adults as our parents remained children.

Consequently, I spent much of my life stoically attempting to control everything, my emotions, my surroundings, the future, and every one around me. I had to learn to let go, to stop trying to master what could not be mastered, to let fate have its way with me, and to accept people the way they are without trying to "fix" them. I needed to learn playfulness, silliness, and innocence-without using alcohol. Authentic children live in the "now", they have short memories, and the future is no farther away than their next meal or television program. Adults have long, deep memories, and are perpetually trying to manage the present and the future. I believe this is why adults, who were allowed or encouraged to become authentic children, find it difficult to understand why we adult children of alcoholics appear completely invested in the past. We experienced our childhood as though we were adults-adults in a child's body. Our childhood was intense, and our behavior always dramatically impacted the entire household. Our "todays" are wished away, and our "tomorrows" are never wished for. The "now's" we lived in were filled with anxiety, apprehension, anger, and fear.

We children of alcoholics were never quiet good enough, invisible enough, or successful enough to heal our parents. We are left with deep wells of sadness and regret because we were never able to make the chaos stop. We survived through powerful anger towards the alcoholic. Anger fills the void where love should be, and a wound is left to fester. I was never able to control my father. He was never able to control himself-yet his alcoholism controlled us all. Therefore my life became perpetually unmanageable, and terrifying.

Our entire family spent our entire life caring for him, waiting on him, and cleaning up after him, encouraging him, calming him, and getting him off to work while taking care of the entire household. He never took care of us. Even during my mother's battles with heart disease, and diabetes her children cared for her not her husband. I fear she died feeling very much alone.

We met every need he ever had. My brothers, sisters, and I became such good enablers we learned to anticipate his every need. We wandered through our lives together like we were walking among sleeping alligators-terrified one false step or slightest noise would cause our demise.

Dad judged our "worthiness" by how well we took care of him. *"Do dear OLE' Dad a favor and...."* If we did well, *"You're a good man Charlie Brown."* Fail and *"cussing, stomping, and sarcasm followed."* Sometimes when I was sent to fetch something, and had returned with it Dad totally ignored me as he continued watching television, or pretending to sleep. I was expected to stand there next to him until recognized. If I interrupted, the alligator would snap. During his illness, with its genuine desperation, all I could think was how weary I had become taking care of him. I had nothing left for him.

My father grew up the only child of the union between a cold manipulative father, and a doting enabling mother. He was an asthmatic child of small stature. This contributed to his mother's smothering servitude of the two men in her household. My father married a woman he hoped would be like his mother and he became perpetually disappointed she did not live up to the standard. My mother gave birth to five children, two girls and three boys. Dad expected his children to fill in the gaps of servitude not provided by his wife or his mother. Whatever our mother did not, or would not do for him, we were expected to do. He expected the entire household to mother him. We had two options confrontation or capitulation. Life became so much easier if we capitulated so we typically did.

We became more like his house staff than his family. Our tasks varied from doing all the yard work and repairs around the house, to bringing him ice cream, changing the TV station, making phone calls, taking messages, and even rubbing his sweaty feet while he slept. Whether he spoke or not he expected us to immediately yield our seat to him as he entered the room. We were required to let him change the TV station without objection. I missed the last half-hour of many movies, and shows.

Mostly we were expected to sit silently. If we left the room we were challenged "What the hell's wrong with you?" It was better never to go into the family room (at all) when Dad was home. We did a lot of hiding in our rooms, the game room in the basement, or better yet get entirely out of the house.

I became a mastermind of passive aggressiveness. If Dad asked for a "soda" (milk and ice cream in a glass) I got it for him but I made sure the glass was slightly covered with ice cream so his hands got sticky. If he turned the television station to a show we all wanted to watch I went to my room and listened to music, just to spite him. If he fell asleep watching the Yankees game I would change the station and sneak off to bed so he never heard the final score.

Dad often complained to us about each other. "What has your brother ever done for me? He has been nothing but a burden?" Or "Your sister is too busy to do anything for me." Every complaint focused on what we were or were not doing for him. In every way we were the adults and he the child. It was as if he was the sun and we were the planets with our orbits dependent entirely on his pull. We were enmeshed in his sick universe. Dad placed value on us based entirely on how well we served him. We were his staff not his children. No kids allowed... Our task is to avoid being enmeshed in other sick relationships.

Patron

After Dad passed away, my brother Ted, my sister Missy, and I spent a long day sorting through his things. It was a mundane exercise until Ted found a letter which forever changed my relationship with my (departed) mother. I loved my mother deeply, and we talked often. She has been dead for several years, and yet I still talk to her. We still have a relationship, and I continue to feel connected to her. *Ma knew me better than anyone else ever did.* As the youngest, I was the last child to escape the nightmare we called home. I am not sure which of us children had the worst experiences. On the occasions when we discuss such issues, I usually conclude we all have had our own unique misery to survive. Yet, the rest of my siblings have a certain commonality of experiences. They seemed to have gone through much of it together, while I felt completely alone.

The letter, we found, was from my mother to my father written while they were still just dating. Most of the letter dealt with my father's drinking. How it was causing problems between them, and how rotten he was to her when he drank. She proposed they start going to the movies instead of going to taverns. Although her complaints were heart-felt, they also felt pathetic to me, and it angered me. *The letter should have been a "Dear John" letter, but instead it was a plea for sobriety.*

The letter devastated me. I had always perceived my mother as a "victim" trapped in an alcoholic marriage. Women of my mother's generation did not get divorced-they often remained in bad marriages. I assumed Mom had been stuck in a terrible marriage and had tried to do her best for her children. In reality, my mother was drawn to an alcoholic, dated an alcoholic, married an alcoholic, and had five children with that same alcoholic. In addition, she stayed with that alcoholic the rest of her life. I came to realize that my mother was a willing participant in the events described in this book. *How could she have loved the alcoholic that was my father?*

My parents argued constantly. Sometimes when they argued mother would threaten to leave Dad, and take the kids with her. Many of these threats were obvious bluffs. On one occasion as they argued Mom told Dad we were all leaving him and she had already made arrangements. Her brother Bob was going to buy a house with an apartment for Mom and us kids. I was so excited that I began to pack a few things.

The part of the plan that was most encouraging was the fact someone outside our household seemed to know what was going on. *Help might be on the way.* The next day it seemed all was forgotten and there was never another mention of it. I am still not sure if Bob ever made the offer or if mother had invented the entire story. We did stay, and mother seemed less and less able to fight or leave. I was stuck, and if I were going to leave, it would be entirely up to me.

I began to keep a notebook with a map to plot my way out. *I was going to run far away.* With my route mapped out I began to save money. The idea was absurd for I knew in my heart I lacked the courage to try, and I never did. I was too afraid of the consequences if I was caught. Most days I was too afraid to leave my room much less leave home. The fantasy (of running away) gave me a few moments of diversion and hope. Mostly I hoped that when I ran someone might realize how terrible my life was and come to my rescue. A hero never came to save me. I was going to have to be my own hero-some day when I was angry enough or discouraged enough not to care about the consequences.

The aspect which can be the most disheartening about living with an alcoholic is the web of secrecy which goes along with this disease. Not only are you in constant fear and pain, you are told that no one can ever know. Implicit is the belief no one already knows. Consequently, we experience desperate loneliness. We carry an ugly secret the world must never know and our belief is if it did, the world would completely reject us. Victims of this web learn the art of minimization and denial when anyone asks what is wrong with us-even within our own family. We act like zombies, and wander through life in a trance of meaningless clichés; *I'm fine-no big deal, nothing is wrong, I'm just tired, or I'd be fine if you all would just leave me alone.* We are able to lie enough to convince ourselves of anything which might get us out of our real feelings of sadness and anger.

Many children of alcoholics feel so deeply abandoned they will accept any love or friendship regardless of how sick or tragic the consequences. Any "bum" who wants to be our friend or companion is welcomed, and cherished. When they're *too* good, we test and distrust them. Often when good things happen to us or good people enter our lives we reject them-so convinced are we they are disingenuous. Consequently, we victims feel completely abandoned and rejected by the world. In my own life, when wonderful things come my way, I always look around for someone trying to take it away. *Good things don't happen to me...* Metaphorically, I am always waiting for the instant replay to overturn the decision, and to find out the touchdown has been disallowed. Children of alcoholics have an ingrained pessimism and a pattern of self-destruction for they believe it is what they deserve.

Through much psychoanalysis, I have learned to identify my self-destructive patterns. This insight helps me to "catch" myself engaging in those patterns and to gradually correct them. I do not believe it would have been possible for me to change these behaviors were it not for my psychiatrist. He was warm and accepting while he guided me through each new insight. I also read many books on the topic of adult children of alcoholics as well as enabling behaviors. These books helped and continue to help me stay focused on corrective behaviors between psychotherapy sessions.

Consequently, I no longer wait for people who love me to hurt or abandon me. I understand conflict is normal and resolutions can be civil. Similarly, I have learned to face conflict, and to stop cowering. I have learned to see my parents as flawed people who, based on their own lifetime of experiences, may have done the best they could.

Furthermore, I have stopped being a perfectionist and caretaker at work: I now see my job as a *negotiable relationship*. I no longer feel the need to control situations or other people. Relying on and trusting people have become easier for me.

I no longer live in fear of what I cannot see or control. Therefore, I am no longer dependent on other people to decide how I feel. My feelings are my own, they not the result of other peoples' actions.

I have learned to forgive my mother. Whatever her reasons for being with my father, they are her own. None of those reasons affected how deeply she loved and cared for her children. Regardless of how hurtful her marriage was she always found love for her children.

I have spent some time learning about my mother's family history, and it has helped a great deal. My mother had her own journey and her own pain. As a result, she may not have believed she deserved a better man than my father. Similarly, women from her generation did not often feel empowered to leave an abusive relationship. For many they just stayed, and hoped for a better tomorrow, and tried to do what they thought was best for their children. My mother and I still talk in our own spiritual way. In some ways, I have never felt closer to her.

Alone in a Crowded Room

It was dusk, and we were playing "army" in the neighborhood woods. The goal of army was to search and destroy your opponent-this night I was the hunted. During the game, I made a fatal mistake as I attempted to move to a better position. While doing so, I spotted the enemy, two friends, walking directly towards me. I stopped right in the worn path of the woods, put my chin into my chest, ceased all movement or breathing, slowed my heart rate down, closed my eyes, and concentrated on the coming darkness. Both of my buddies walked right passed me and never saw me, or even sensed my presence. I had become invisible.

I was an expert at invisibility, *Don't worry about me I'm fine...* I was relegated to the shadowlands of my family, often dismissed, and rarely accounted for. I did not have enough problems to matter much to anyone. Watching horror movies, I empathized with hunted characters: the ones who were being chased, or watched by some unknown evil presence. The part that baffled me was their inability to hide. *I knew how to hide.* I knew how to become my own black hole, suck all the light in, and become invisible.

Sometimes I just sat in the back corner of my closet and pulled piles of clothing all around me. I sat there quietly feeling safe and protected knowing no one could find me. No one could intrude on this quiet moment-other times I crawled under my bed camouflaged by boxes, craving peace and safety. Some of the most liberating moments of my childhood came during those rare times when I was home alone. This euphoric feeling of perfect contentment usually ended with a long peaceful sleep. Time spent home alone, and napping are still some of my most contented moments.

Insanity and fear were the monsters in our house. There was so much insanity floating around the house it took something truly bizarre for me to even be noticed. I was always the one no one worried about-compared to the rest; I seemed to be doing fine. *Danny was quiet and never seemed to cause a fuss-he must be fine. He's not the one we worry about.* Everyone seemed to have a glazed look on their faces. It reminded me of robbers wearing stocking masks to conceal their identity. These glazed faces even haunted my sleep.

I had one terrible repetitive nightmare. The dream takes place on a second floor flat we rented until I was about eight years old. During the dream it is night, and I am awakened by noises. I get out of bed to investigate. The lights are on and the kitchen door, leading to the stairway, is wide open. No one else seems to be in the apartment so I tried to peer out of the misty kitchen window to look for them. I kneel down and start to rub the window glass with my pajama shirtsleeve. I squint and stare out trying to see down to the street. There seems to be a crowd around my Dad's car parked across the sidewalk. I recognize my brothers and sisters being hurried into our car. I am being left all alone. Just as I start to get a clearer view it is blocked by an image of my father's laughing face looking into the house from the other side of the glass. *This is impossible; I am on the second floor...* I rub another spot on the window glass and the image of my (paternal) grandmother's laughing face appears. Panicked, I rub frantically spot after spot, until the entire window if filled with their laughing faces. When I awoke from the dream I had the desperate feelings of loneliness and vulnerability. I am alone and frightened, yet I feel ridiculous.

The very people who are supposed to protect me chose instead to ridicule me, and to laugh at my vulnerability. I was alone and terrified with no one to help or console me. I awoke frightened, angry, and frustrated. They were leaving me, and I was left completely abandoned-except for the monsters. The dream was similar to the nightmare I was living.

I still feel as I did in that dream-abandoned. I continue to have great difficulty sharing my pain or asking for help. I act as if I am all alone no matter how many people care about me. I assume people are unreliable, my worries are mine alone. *My fears are a joke, and I am alone with them.* This attitude has caused problems in all my relationships, but particularly in my marriage.

My wife ends up shut out of my feelings and problems. When these feelings escape, they manifest themselves in disproportionate and hysterical ways. She is left wondering what happened, and I am left resentful of her lack of understanding. I feel I am still the little boy (in my dream) looking out the window and wondering why everyone is sneaking off to without me, completely abandoned, terrified, and helpless.

One of our best conversations took place after my wife read a few rough draft chapters of this book. It was the first time my suffering became tangible to her, and she truly felt some of the pain I carry. Andrea wrote me a note expressing how sad my pain had made her and how deeply she wished I had not suffered so much. I keep the note on the table next to our bed. It helps me to not feel so alone.

We, the survivors of alcoholic parents are not alone there are millions of us. We are your friends, co-workers, entertainers, and even world leaders. All of us share the same hole in our soul. This emptiness creates a longing, a hunger for love, gentleness, and simple kindness. We are looking for peace, the kind of peace found in a loved person's soul, the kind of peace most consider merely "normal." Although we push everyone away-hold us close, tell us it will be all right, be patient with us, and love us a little more for we feel afraid and alone.

Stranger

In an alcoholic home, everyone's feelings are completely dependent upon the alcoholic themselves. So desperate are we for peace and sanity we are willing to dance the dance of the alcoholic as they set the tune.

While slightly intoxicated my Dad could be confident, talkative, and playful. A couple of drinks later he could be bitter, judgmental, and confrontational. When fully intoxicated he was manipulative, cruel, and sometimes violent. We argued, laughed, or hid in response to whatever mood the alcohol had induced. My family lived a dance macabre with a drunk leading.

When he was not out drinking or at work Dad was home and sick from drinking. During his hangover phase, we were expected to be servants who tended to his every whim. We were expected to act as if he were the victim of some terrible illness, rather than recovering from his own weakness and negligence.

During his daily hangovers Dad slept in his bathrobe on the living room sofa. Dad lay there for hours at a time, *sleeping it off*, snoring, and reeking of body and foot odor. He demanded the television be on and tuned to the show he wanted to see, even while he slept. If he awoke and "his show" was not on, Dad would curse at us, and criticize us for "watching that shit." If he awoke and his show was on, he'd often command one of us to get him ice cream, or milk and cookies for him. Other times he would order me to scratch his feet.

I sat on the end of the couch with his sweaty, smelly feet in my lap as I was told to rub and scratch them. I was expected to continue even after he fell back asleep. There was little chance of getting off the couch without waking him. On rare occasions, I was able to move a little bit at a time, imperceptibly, and sneak away. I needed to go right to bed in an attempt to avoid his wrath when he noticed I was gone. My Dad and his alcoholism were in complete control of my life. My life was out of control long after Dad stopped drinking. Alcoholism continues to constantly dominate my life.

I have spent most of my life letting others control how I act and how I feel. If people are angry, I walk around on little cat feet, and try to console them. If they are happy, I celebrate with them and tell them how much they deserve to be happy. I am quick to apologize even if I am the victim. I am an expert at covering up for other people, and making excuses for them. I let everyone off the hook, except for myself. I have spent a lifetime swallowing my true feelings.

People who are calm and composed during tragedies or emergencies seem alien to me. I have both admired and resented them. Their self-control seems phony and contrived. The feeling I have had the most difficulty touching, and expressing is joy. When I watch a sporting event, and my team scores, I wait for the instant replay before I believe it has happened. I always anticipate some external force will take every good thing I have from me-not just every good thing, but all the people I love. Part of my obsessive-compulsive disorder is an overwhelming fear that a tragedy will injure or kill my children.

I love my children. They are exactly what I dreamed children would be. In many ways, they hold my hopes and dreams. I cannot wait to see what wonderful things they will do with the rest of their lives. Yet, in a dark part of my brain I feel as though I am not worthy of this happiness. I worry obsessively their pure goodness is temporary and will be taken away from me. *My love for them and their love for me are so pure, innocent it must be associated with tragedy, and sadness-it is only a matter of time until they are lost to me.* I do not deserve the happiness they bring me.

With fear perched on the edge of my consciousness, I have spent years compulsively protecting my children. While they played outside, I constantly checked on them. If they were in the front yard I jumped every time I heard a car approach, so convinced was I a random car would swerve off the road onto our lawn and kill them. If they were in the backyard I worried some hunter's stray shot would hit them. At night, I never slept deeply, often listening to every little noise. I was ever vigilant in protecting my children. If a car went by and I did not clearly hear it pass by, I needed to get up and go to the window to reassure myself the car had not stopped and was not lurking in front of my house. I imagined people sneaking around the outside of the house looking in the windows at my children. Every one of my children's coughs or groans needed my immediate personal attention. My son suffered from colic and cried himself to sleep many nights. This worried me so much that to get any sleep at all I had to sleep on the floor next to his crib. It seemed to sooth both of us. Many mornings my wife found me asleep and shivering on the floor.

Alone each of these precautions may seem like I was just a concerned parent living in a dangerous world. Together they amount to mental illness. I had everything in life I ever hoped for, and yet I was incapable of enjoying it. I was constantly on guard trying to protect it all. I had no joy in my life. I was a walking corpse taken out of a George Romero film. I was afraid if I were too happy, my life and my loves would be taken from me.

I have come to understand through psychotherapy, and through self-education my obsessive-compulsive disorder (OCD) is a symptom or result of post-traumatic stress disorder (PTSD). Many people associate PTSD with traumatic events survived in wartime, but Psychiatry have concluded PTSD can happen to anyone who suffers prolong trauma such as physical or emotional abuse. My OCD (repetitive behaviors and obsessive thoughts) help me to control my anxiety in a limited/temporary way. Of course these obsessions and compulsions just prolong and ingrain those same anxieties. In the end the anxiety stockpiles until it overwhelms. These increased anxieties merely provoke more obsessions and compulsions. Additionally, prolonged exposure to inescapable anxiety increases the production of adrenaline and this lowers serotonin levels in the brain. The long-term result is sufferers of PTSD become behaviorally, and chemically less able to handle stress. This self-perpetuating cycle generated my mental illness, and cripples many others.

I often jumped in paralyzing fear at the sound of a car approaching my home. High speeds were especially troublesome. The sound of a vehicle coming in my driveway caused constant panic attacks. Psychiatric insight has helped me to touch the source of this debilitating tension. The noises put me in a car with my drunken father driving. I associate car noises with paralyzing fear. In addition, my anxiety over my children's safety is really a reliving of my own trepidation as a child. I was reliving my own traumatic experiences through my children.

These fears dissipated shortly after entering therapy. Thoroughly understanding my illness has helped me control it. I also spent a few months taking a sedative in the afternoon, my most anxious time of the day. This mild sedative taught me what "normal" felt like. I learned it was not normal to spend every day with a headache, tightness in my chest, and a rapid heartbeat. Normal was sweet and good. I began to experience joy, and control over my emotions for the first time in my life. I enjoyed my children; I laughed with my wife, and at myself. I found work to be challenging not worrisome. I fell asleep quickly, and slept deeply. I did not need large doses of caffeine to stay awake throughout the day. I felt normal and alive!

My struggles with Depression and PTSD will continue for the rest of my life. Keeping my mental health is like trying to contain an oil spill in the ocean. Unless I am consistently working the spill, it is bound to slip away. Sometimes I just find myself at the bottom of a pit of despair, and I have no idea how I got there. It is a maddening feeling because I had convinced myself I felt good-yet here I am, in darkness.

My depression feels like I have a shield around my face so I can only see what is directly in front of me. This shield narrows imperceptibly every day. Everything blindsides me. My life is slowly slipping out of control. My only defense it to be increasingly vigilant and defensive. I am easily angered, self-involved, and hypersensitive to my environment. Everything/every one drives me crazy. I feel like a corpse lying still as the worms eat away my flesh. Finally, I see it-I am sick. I am depressed.

My psychiatrist and I began to work on a new plan with an adjustment in medication, and some reprogramming of self-defeating habits. After a few weeks, I realized just how ill I was feeling as I touched wellness again. I felt safe for a while longer. You have no idea just how sick you are until you feel well, then you are shocked how ill you really were. It is all part of the fight for mental health many survivors go through every day.

Keeping a Tab

For the first twenty years of my life, I lived with my
family in a lower flat of an up-and-down apartment house.
Although my parents ended up living there for a total of
about thirty years, we behaved as though we would be forced
to move at any moment. We always did electrical and
plumbing repairs in a patchwork fashion to not *fix it for the
next tenant.* Calling the landlord for repairs seemed out of
the question; *he'll just raise the rent.* To sign a rental lease
was unthinkable, *just in case we wanted to move.* If we ever
spotted the landlord checking on the property, my parents
assumed it meant the property was for sale. *Surely the new*

owners would want us out. This caused a few weeks worth of panic.

The flat was dark. The walls were smoke-stained khaki green, the carpet hunter green, and furniture brown. The windows had thick tobacco stained curtains. Lights were few, and rarely turned on to save electricity. The lampshades were so soiled the light which passed through resembled bug light yellow. When the furniture became worn, we covered them with slips. The rugs were never cleaned and only the kitchen floor was ever washed. Our bathroom was always shedding tiles, and all the plumbing fixtures leaked. I never thought of us poor, but we were.

If compared to any technical measurement of wealth we would likely have been ranked as lower middle class, but Dad left a great deal of his check at the Alpine Village Tavern. We were never hungry or homeless. On the other hand, my parents never had a dime in the bank, and we owned nothing new. Everything in our house was used: furniture, dishes, televisions, clothes, beds, and even bikes all second hand. We never went to the doctor or dentist unless it was an emergency. My brothers and I all have terrible teeth, and I still feel guilty *wasting money* on a doctor even when I am sick.

All of the kids worked part-time jobs as soon as we were able, and each of us paid a portion of it back to our parents for room and board. In fact, for many years, even Mom worked part-time to make a little extra money. We could never make money as fast as Dad could drink it.

Daily problems like poor grades, repairs, arguments, relationships, and chores were largely ignored. The person who owned the problem handled it alone, and quietly. We never sought help, and never talked to anyone about it. Large problems like raised rents, job changes, arrests, or serious illness completely paralyzed everyone with fear and anxiety. It was like being on a plane and discovering no landing gear or pilot existed. Everything seemed out of our control.

Typically, Dad would handle bigger problems by sitting at the kitchen table, smoking cigarettes, and making lists. Nothing on those lists was ever acted upon, and typically, he sought his kids out for advice. Mostly he wished it all away.

My family was incredibly stoic. We could stare down the Sphinx. None of us ever mentioned Dad's drinking-even to each other. I cannot recall one single conversation about his drinking with any of my siblings.

Ironically, during the years when my brother Ted was drinking, it was Ted's drinking (never Dad's) that consumed our conversations. Dad's umbrage at Ted's drinking just angered Ted, and made his reliance on alcohol worsen. In our sick dysfunctional dance, Ted became the focus of our family's shame. Sadly, my father seemed to revel in Ted's downward spiral of alcoholism. In a way, Mom and Dad seemed to grow closer as they worked together on Ted's alcohol related problems.

Collectively we solved none of life's problems. Life happened to us, and every good turn was met with suspicion, as if it were a lucky break, similarly every bad turn was perceived as hard luck. We took responsibility for nothing. We were a hard luck family, and everyone seemed against us. We were taught to trust no one, and expect help from no one. It became "us against the world." Yet, there was no "us" as we were truly alone.

For years when faced with problems I got a terrible feeling of loneliness and despair. I seemed unable to ask for help, and tended to drown in self-pity. I trusted few people completely, and tended to try to handle challenges alone. It has taken many years of retraining to learn to recognize those feelings and to overcome them.

Here is what I have learned... I'll call it a "Problem Solving" checklist for Adult Children of Alcoholics."

1. People like to help-especially when asked.
2. Problems are rarely as big as you imagine them to be.
3. Having difficulty is not a reflection of your toughness.
4. Just because somebody has it worse doesn't mean you are not in pain.
5. Everybody has problems and they overcome them all the time.
6. It is ok to pay professionals for their expertise, don't feel guilty-you are worth it.
7. Get in touch with and trust your instincts.
8. Not all problems can be fixed, they may just have to be survived.
9. Nobody is keeping score.

10. Sometimes no amount of planning could have prevented the problem from happening so... "Get off your Back!"

11. Pray and ask God for strength and wisdom.

Good Times

In the summers of my childhood, our family joined several other families for a week at Bobs Lake in rural Ontario, Canada. The week was spent swimming, fishing, and playing games. The standard bearer of this trip was my father's best friend William Francis Hoctor-everyone called him Franny. His children and their families were the core of our stay at Morter's Camp on Bob's Lake. My family was more of an invited guest.

Franny was a small, wiry Irishman, a World War II veteran, a former semi-pro football player, a supreme storyteller, and a drinker. To me he was a "man's man." His wife Minerva, though a small lean woman, gave Franny all he could handle. Although I was only a kid I noticed she wore stylish sporty ensembles, always had her hair just so, with a little bit of an alcohol induced "buzz" on. Minerva and my mother were best pals as well. When Franny aggravated "Nerve" she quietly mumbled insults with her raspy smoker's voice, bringing a hefty laugh from my mother.

Our trip to Bob's Lake held more anticipation for me than Christmas morning. I spent hours getting my fishing tackle in order. Although I never had much in my tackle box, what I did have was important to me. One year, while in a bait shop, I discovered a detailed map of the lake, and purchased it. From then on, I spent weeks staring at the map looking for hidden inlets and coves that would potentially be fishing holes. I only tested one two of these spots for I only fished when someone would take me, and we usually went to their favorite fishing spots. There was complete joy in imagining I might get to one of my secret spots, actually catch fish, and impress everyone. Maybe the men would gather around and ask me where the spot was and how I had found it. Maybe they would listen to me tell the story like they listened to Franny tell his stories.

Bob's Lake was about six hours from our home in Buffalo, but it was a whole day adventure. Our trip was initially a clean and sober adventure. With other people along, my parents were on their best behavior. Along the way, our caravan of cars stopped at restaurants, visited souvenir shops, and shared real family moments. The nearest town to Bob's Lake was a wonderful little tourist stop named Westport, our final stop before we arrived at Morter's Camp.

Upon arriving in Westport we split into three groups: the women went shopping at the supermarket for a few forgotten items, the men went to a local pub to drink beer and talk about the driving, and the kids flocked to souvenir and bait tackle shops where we spent what few dollars we had saved up. There were two shops we kids ran to, a five and dime general store, and a fishing tackle shop. At the five and ten, we bought a few trinkets but more importantly a few packs of firecrackers. The tackle shop was full of exotic-looking lures which were just as likely to frighten the fish as to attract them. By the time we arrived at the tackle store, I had typically spent all my money on firecrackers. After rummaging through that shop, we rarely bought anything. We usually fished with worms anyway.

Subsequently, the women would grumble back from shopping at the unfamiliar grocery store. They would ask, "Where's your father?" to any one of us who was listening. One of us would motion to the pub, and off they would go to drag them out.

We had one last important stop, the Beer Store. In Canada, beer is purchased in a separate store. The Beer Store had an "in" sign and an "out" sign in front, so the locals all called it the "In and Out" Store." It was only another ten miles to Morter's Camp but the roads were largely dirt and narrow. To avoid return trips to Westport, everyone stocked up on beer in Westport on the way in to Morter's Camp. Each family purchased approximately eight cases of beer, and jammed them into their already overloaded cars. Being a kid, I usually sat on top of two or three cases for the remaining miles of the trip. About mid-week the men would return to the "In and Out" to restock. I figure each adult drank about a case of beer a day. They drank from morning until late into the evening, slowly but constantly.

The winding dirt roads added to my feeling of adventure. When we finally arrived at Morter's Camp, the men would sit around the outdoor picnic tables and discuss the drive while opening a few more cold ones. The women and children unpacked, set up the cabin, fetched water from the well, and got dinner started. After dinner, the older kids would fetch their family's rented motor from the lodge, claim their rented boats, and ready them. If we were lucky, we might get out for a short boat ride before bedtime. Our vacation would not begin in earnest until the following morning.

I felt safe in the cabins at Morter's Camp. The walls were thin and the floors were bare allowing sound to travel easily through the campground. Therefore, my parents were hesitant to behave too badly. Arguments were kept down, and since we kids were always off playing somewhere, we did not hear many of them. Quite often, we shared a cabin with Franny, Minerva, and their son Kevin who was the same age I was. Their presence kept things a little calm. Mom and Dad were always more considerate towards friends and strangers than to their own family. I always felt safe around Franny because he would speak up to protect a kid. Franny consistently looked out for me, and a little part of me wondered and/or dreamed he was my real father.

I loved waking to the quiet and safety of Bob's Lake. Many mornings I lay awake in bed and listened to the waves, the distant sound of boats, or to the quiet conversations of fishermen on the docks plotting their strategy for the day.

Usually I was able to sit and eat breakfast with Franny as he sat and drank tea for hours. It seemed he always had something positive and funny to say. Soon afterwards Kevin and I wandered around outside to see if anyone was going out fishing. Kevin was annoyingly bold and would just ask if he could tag along. I was pathetically shy, and hoped somebody would invite me along. Most of the time, they failed to notice my subtle hints and I stayed behind. I would jealously watch Kevin go and I'd find a place to go and sulk. I might convince myself the boat docks were a good enough place to fish from, and fetch my pole, or I might find a good hiding spot in the rock formations near the lake, sit, and read comic books.

The biggest thrill was if Franny's son-in-law Gary let me tag along fishing with him. Gary was quiet, intelligent, and a very serious fisherman. When I fished with him, he would talk to me about history, nature, and even philosophy. He seemed remarkably interested in what I thought about those topics. Occasionally, Gary would let me drive the boat home. I never wanted those fishing trips to end.

Usually around noon, the adults began to gather on the docks or at the picnic tables near the water edge. They exchanged stories, argued politics, laughed, and supervised the kids as they played in the sand or at the edge of the water. They all had a beer in one hand and a cigarette in the other. After all, they were on vacation too… it was all harmless fun. The afternoons were the best of times. Many days Franny's two son-in-laws Gary and Chuck would run their boat for water skiing. Rooting for whomever was skiing; watching whatever tricks they could do was terrific fun for all. At twelve years of age, I was able to finally get up on the skis and I loved it. Chuck and Gary would spend the entire afternoon helping everyone ski. They reserved the last rides of the day for themselves. They were excellent skiers and put on a real show. I often sat and wished I would become just like them.

By late afternoon, all the adults were quiet and intoxicated. Each family would go back to their cabins for dinner. My parents seemed especially irritated at this time of the day. Mom was resentful she had to cook while on vacation. Dad was already pretty drunk and aggravated that he had to stop drinking to eat. Usually both were angry about something someone else had said or done that afternoon. The best I could hope for was they were both angry with the same person; this seemed to ally them and create the most peaceful situation.

After dinner, my Dad took a nap to get ready for the evening of drinking while Mom sat outside and worked on a crossword puzzle or talked with Minerva. I hung around the adults to see if anyone was going fishing. At dusk, the adults gathered at a pre-arranged cabin for a party. The evening often began with a poker game and ended with songs or laughs. The kids were allowed to hang out and even join in. It was terrific fun to see my parents having such a good time. They were both very drunk, very silly, and often the center of attention. This was as close as we came to a happy family all year long.

If they could have found their way home before they were fully intoxicated, it would have been a perfect night. My father could not force himself to leave before he had gone too far. He was always the last one to leave, sometimes at the host's request. If the party were at our cabin, he and

Franny would sit at the table and argue on almost any topic until one or both passed out at the table. If Dad passed out first Franny would often sit and continue to talk to him, as if he was still awake. If the talking kept Mom awake she would often come out of her room and pick a fight. It was during these times my parents would have their worst arguments.

Both intoxicated, and without inhibitions, there was no limit to how cruel they could be to each other. My mother would accuse Dad of being a "Momma's boy", Dad would call her a "fat ass", Mom would talk about how lousy he was in bed, Dad countered with accusations some of the kids were not his. Hearing the fighting through the thin walls of the cabin, I spent many nights falling asleep with tears in my eyes. Sometimes I really hated Bobs Lake.

Spending time with my family was often the last thing I wanted to do at Bobs Lake. Contentment for me was being alone in a quiet place, safe from chaos, in complete control, fantasizing about what kind of life I could make for myself someday. I would sit on top of a hill in the long grass and stare longingly at some distant inlet, dreaming of the peaceful cabin I might live in some day. Sometimes I'd take a long walk down a dirt road lost in thoughts and aspirations. I lived inside my own imagination.

The last day of our week at the lake was full of overwhelming melancholy; I never wanted to return to the world I had briefly escaped from. Some years all the families caravanned back home together. This seemed to prolong our vacation just a touch longer. The last few years everyone else stayed for two weeks but we did not. This resulted is an especially dark ride home. My mother never wanted to stay for two weeks. She claimed there were other places she wanted to go during the second week of my father's vacation time, although we never went anywhere.

The year my brother Marty got married, my parents announced they could not afford a wedding and a vacation in the same year. Accordingly, we were not going to Bob's Lake. I was terrified; all my instincts told me that if my parents skipped a year we would never return. On the last day of vacation each year, everyone paid their bill, and locked-up reservations for the following year. If we were ever going back, my parents would have to make their own reservations. I knew they were not capable of taking the initiative or responsibility for that. My instincts were right, we never returned as a family; our days at Morter's Camp were over.

Franny rescued me that year when he offered to take me along with his family. To my great surprise, Mom and Dad said I could go. This was to be my best trip ever at Bob's Lake. For one week of my life, I had a real father. Franny treated me like a son and I learned to treat him as a father. When I was wrong, he quietly corrected me, and when I was right he encouraged me. He gave me chores to do and expected me to be a man and do them. He took me fishing and let me drive the boat. Franny even asked other people if they would take "Danny along fishing." I could not wait to please him; I even looked for extra chores to do, cleared the table after dinner, did the dishes, put his gear in the boat, stocked a couple of beers in the cooler for him, asked to hear war stories, and made tea for him. The feeling of safety and joy was so overwhelming I often had to stop myself from weeping. I would have made a great son.

I have returned a couple of times with my own family, but it never had the same magic. Bobs Lake no longer needed to fill an empty place in me. It was merely a quiet little lake in Ontario, Canada. It had not changed a bit; I had changed a great deal. The sad and lonely boy of my youth had made his dreams come true, and no longer needed to escape to Bobs Lake, and his own imagination to find peace.

One for the Road

My wife and I were recently returning home from an evening of shopping. I was driving, and my wife sat next to me in the passenger seat. Suddenly a man driving an old brown car, with a noisy muffler, swerved and cut us off. Looking over the back seat out the rear window of his car was a little boy with big blue eyes gazing out longingly. He looked right at me, and ours eyes locked. The two little pools of blue in his eyes seemed sad and alone. I felt like he wanted me to rescue him. The car cut over two more lanes and made a turn. I could barely breathe as my hands squeezed the steering wheel and my heart pounded. I felt like I wanted to cry and giggle all at once.

I had become the little boy with the longing blue eyes. I was in the back seat with him... coming home from my Uncle Al's with both parents drunk. I was unknowingly suffering from Post-Traumatic Stress Syndrome, and having a flashback.

Throughout most of my childhood, my entire family went to my Uncle Al's and Aunt Betty's every sunny, summer, Sunday afternoon. Aunt Betty needed to stay home. I suppose today we would call her agoraphobic. Conversely, Uncle Al loved to be the life of the party. So they compromised, and had a huge redwood pool installed. Next, they invited all their friends to their home every Sunday in June, July, and August. All their friend's kids swam in the pool, rode bikes in the driveway, or played games in the basement. The women watched as the kids swim, sat, talked, and drank. Meanwhile, the men pitched rubber horseshoes in the driveway, ate clams, and drank.

At Uncle Al's house I became independent and playful. My parents were so preoccupied they left me alone. I loved going off riding a bike or shooting pool in the basement- solitude embraced me. When I was alone it felt peaceful, serene, and safe. In the early evenings, as the sky turned amber, I became both excited and frightened. Uncle Al always seemed to have a few fireworks to light, and a few flares to spark as kids all pulled up lawn chairs and watched. While enjoying the fireworks display I became increasingly agitated by the paralyzing fear of the coming ride home, and wondered if we would get home alive.

My father drove a beat up red Ford convertible with a noisy muffler. Most Sundays, as he drove us home, curses and shouts went back and forth in the front seat between my drunken parents. Not only was the driver drunk, he was also fully distracted. During these rides Dad missed stop signs, swerved around parked cars, barely avoided pedestrians, and cussed at my mother as well as the other drivers. On occasion he even turned into driveways (at 20-30 mph) mistaking them for streets. There were times when we got lost on the way home. To my permanent amazement he never did kill us, or get stopped by the police.

On the wild rides home from Uncle Al's I cowered in the backseat, frozen, silently pretending to drive, making each turn, concentrating, sending mental messages (to Dad) warning of oncoming traffic or red lights, willing us home. I sometimes counted to ten hoping to live just ten more seconds, ten more, and ten more.

Much of my life has been accompanied by similar paralyzing fear. It is a familiar companion, and I have become accustomed to the rapid heart rate and the churning stomach. The epitome of my anxiety, and my personal motto became "The disasters I do not imagine are the one which will get me." In short, I had to prepare for every possible negative scenario to prevent bad things from happening. It seemed to me optimism and innocence was signs of weakness and a failure of preparation. I existed prepared for every possible catastrophe in the hopes of avoiding them. Mostly I focused and ruminated on worst-case scenarios. This was how I maintained control, and it was part of the germination of my obsessive-compulsiveness.

The flashback, that put me in the backseat, with the little blue-eyed boy, made me realize (for the first time) just how ill I was, and how unlikely it was going change without help. Shortly after that flashback I sought professional help.

Control is a rare luxury for a child of an alcoholic; most often other people control us. We are satellites and the alcoholics are the orbs we circle, pulled in by their neediness, and victimization. As mere satellites, we are completely dependent on the alcoholic for our sense of who we are. If they allow light to pass, we reflect it, if they block the light we exist in darkness. Yet we seem incredibly powerless to leave our familiar orbit. This describes my experiences with codependence.

Children of alcoholics are so dependent they need laugh tracks to know when it is appropriate to be joyful. Spontaneity is numbed out of us as it frightens us so. Even our sadness is expressed inappropriately. We seem to be unable to cry at funerals; yet we sob uncontrollably during a standing ovation. Overall, we possess little understanding of "normal" behavior. Many of us become jealous and resentful of normal children who worry about stupid petty things like homework or baseball. We spend much of our lives trying to find a place to live between numbness and chaos. Many of us use chemicals or compulsions to create our own chaos or to numb out our anxiety. Others of us build relationships with people who are more ill than we are to feel superior or useful.

Waves of indescribable sadness pour over us and melt us like an ice sculpture on a summer day. Nothing needs to happen to bury us in these feelings. Many of us have common emotional triggers which precede these overwhelming feelings of sadness or anxiety. Some of our triggers are subconscious, like my swerving car experience, while others are quite recognizable. Although we recognize some of the triggers we are powerless to prevent their inevitable affects. I now understand erratically driven automobiles and vehicles with loud mufflers trigger paralyzing anxiety in me. Through therapy and the love of my family, I have learned to let these triggers pass over me without automatically raising my anxiety. I am no longer victimized by the imagined dangers these triggers cause me to re-live. Sedatives have helped me to re-associate those triggers to calmness and safety. Automatic responses no longer direct my feelings and behaviors.

Uncle Al died suddenly of a heart attack in 1975. I loved him dearly, and think of him often. For a while, Aunt Betty tried to keep the Sunday tradition going but it was never the same. After a year we stopped going entirely. We spent our Sunday's home with everyone going off in different directions.

Many Sundays, Dad would take his mother to church and stop at a tavern afterwards. He usually arrived home just before dinner, fought with Mom, gagged his dinner up, and slept the evening away on the couch. Many Sundays I rode my bicycle to friend's homes where they did things together as a family. Sometimes I was included, other times I was sent away. As a result, I spent most Sundays trying to stay occupied and quiet alone in my room-hiding from the anger and insanity of own home.

Cook

Tenderness came to me in small helpings-like a sinfully sweet dessert, and I savor the memories of those rare moments. These memories remind me of how sweet life can be. These flashes of kindness filled me with hope, love, and a longing for better days.

Once or twice a year, between the ages of 4 to 10, I was invited to spend a weekend with my maternal Grandmother. Since being widowed in 1962, Grandma Cook lived with, and was cared for by her son (my Uncle) Bob. Bob appeared to be rigid, firm, distant, and cold, and I was afraid of him. Bob was somewhat of a stranger to me for I most often stayed with Grandma Cook when Bob was out of town.

Typically, I stayed in Bob's room, a tidy little room where I slept among his papers and books. Every item in his room had its own place and space. It was like sleeping in a

72

library-quite different from the chaos of my own home. I did not understand at the time I was visiting not only to see Grandma, but also to watch over her while Bob was away. She had "sugar" and became confused if her diabetes flared and her blood sugar levels dropped. It really was a wonderful arrangement for us both. We took care of each other.

Grandma was a chubby woman with hair dyed shiny blue, and a sweet slow voice decorated by a gentle smile. Grandma always wore airy blue housedresses, with lightweight sweaters buttoned up the front. I am sure they fit her once, but not in quite a while. Now she wore them unbuttoned with tissues pushed up her sleeves. Her hands and legs swollen and tired from her diabetes were gentle and beautiful to me. Her gout legs were so painful she had to hold on to furniture in order to walk around the house.

Grandma loved to cook and often wore an apron. The apron pockets were secretly loaded with Captain Crunch cereal she nibbled on all day long. Sweets were strictly of limits, but we all pretended not to notice her hands sneaking into her apron pockets.

Grandma and Uncle Bob had a comedic relationship. Bob was a little stiff and rigid in his ways, and Grandma seemed to enjoy irritating him just a tad knowing he needed to loosen up a bit. For example, Grandma drove Uncle Bob to distraction by always starting dinner in the late morning hours. Bob was a high school Social Studies teacher, and was always home before 5pm. Even at an early hour, dinner was always overcooked and dry.

Grandma and I spent many hours' playing card games, and I always won. Rummy and crazy eights were our two favorite games. *I must have been an exceptional player (for my age) because I always stuck her with a fistful of points.* We played for a nickel a game with money she gave me, and she always had a new deck of cards for me to take home.

On Saturday nights, we watched the CBS comedy lineup (All in the Family, The Jeffersons, The Mary Tyler Moore Show, The Bob Newhart Show, and of course-our favorite-The Carol Burnett Show.) We laughed together for three hours. She had a great hearty laugh which caused her to rock faster in her rocking chair as her stomach jiggled up and down. I laughed more at her laughter than I did at the television shows. It was a special evening of fun if Tim

Conway was on The Carol Burnett Show. Grandma loved him and got beside herself laughing at him. My sides would hurt from laughing at Grandma laughing at him.

I always took a nap at Grandma's house, even long after I had stopped taking them at home. *She took a nap in her chair so why shouldn't I take one too?* I loved sleeping at Grandma's house. Her home had the hush of a law library. The air was filled with the smell of pot roasts cooking or casseroles bubbling. I felt safe, peaceful, loved, and contented around her. Sleep was never so satisfying as it was at Grandma's house. Grandma Cook seemed to want to take care of me, and genuinely enjoyed my company. She told me I was funny, smart, and handsome, and told me she loved me-like no one else ever had.

One visit was especially memorable. I was about six when my parents went to New York City for a few days while I stayed with both Grandma and Uncle Bob. Each night we three dressed for dinner and ate in the dining room. We all watched television together, and then Grandma would tuck me into her bed. I never thought about where she had slept-likely in her chair. At home I was never tucked in, and no one else ever sat on the edge of the bed talking sweetly to me until my eyelids started to drop, but Grandma did. In her room I felt surrounded by her and her tenderness. The bed smelled like her and it seemed as though I was in her arms as I slept. On the last night of this visit I became so overwhelmed by my love for her I wept into her pillow. I sobbed in my own pillow the next night thinking how much I already missed her.

She died when I was 25 years old. I think of her often with love and wonder. I wonder if she knew just how much I needed her or how much I loved her. I was not very good at telling people how I felt. I loved her so deeply she must have felt it.

It was only after Grandma Cook passed we all came to realize the burden Bob had been shouldering by caring for her. He had devoted most of his adult life to her-never marrying. No longer having to care for Grandma allowed Bob to express a friendlier and warmer part of him. Recently I have welcomed him as a member of my own family, and he is completely dedicated to my children. Since my own mother's passing, Bob has become my only connection to her family, and I feel closer to Ma and Grandma when he is with us.

Waiter

Children in an alcoholic home disconnect from reality. They are told so many lies they accept lying as a perpetual method of survival. *Dad's not drunk, he's sick. Don't pay attention to what Dad said he doesn't know what he's saying. He didn't mean to hit me/you. Don't be so sensitive.* The worst lie of all is pretending traumatic events never happened.

Imagine you are a waiter in an elegant restaurant. A waiter's job is to serve the guests, to help them feel good, and to have a pleasant experience regardless of how their day was. A skillful waiter is supposed to be polite, demure, and accommodating no matter how rude or condescending the guests are. The waiter's problems (there are many) are their own. It would be inappropriate for the waiter to share his frustrations with the customers or let them affect his demeanor with the customers. If he should fall, spill, react angrily, tell a customer "no," or fail to please, he is reprimanded. If the waiter completes all these tasks with a good nature, he may receive a token reward. This is what it felt like growing up in my alcoholic home.

I was taught to be a fraud. To pretend everything was good, no matter how bad it felt. My primary job involved making everyone else feel good regardless of how I felt. After a while I no longer knew how I felt. At home the biggest sin one could commit was to act "inappropriately" or have a "poor" attitude. If I danced this phony dance well, I occasionally got rewarded. If I danced poorly, I was decisively beaten down with shame and humiliation.

In this barrage of defense mechanisms, the truth is destroyed because it causes everyone else too much pain. Everything is "swept under the rug." An elephant has been swept under the rug, and there is a big lump in the middle of the living room.

Regardless of what horror or violence happened the night before, my family began every day as if it were merely a normal day. There were no apologies, amends, regrets, or even acknowledgements we had all suffered something horrific the previous night. We walked and talked like zombies-little "Stepford Wives." We ate breakfast with polite and inane conversations. We exchanged our "good-byes" and "have a good days" with feigned sincerity.

In elementary school I developed a theory, and it seemed to help me understand my parents' bizarre behavior. Actually it was more than a theory, I believed it.   I rationalized I had two sets of parents: a calm and rational set, and an angry set. I deduced the two sets freely changed off, and while one set was on duty the other was sent went away for some kind of training. I confided this idea to another kid in the neighborhood, and he began watching his own parents for signs they had switched with their "body doubles." It got so we could tell by looking at our parents which set they were. This theory seemed to explain a great deal of the bizarre behavior I witnessed.

My idea gained validity when my friend told me his Mom had blamed some mild forgetfulness on her "identical twin." I'm sure she had no idea why her son screamed and ran across the street. This science fiction fantasy seemed to make a great deal more sense to me than the dysfunctional reality I was living with.

When alcohol is involved it becomes easy to wonder who your parents really are. After one drink they are silly and playful, after a few more they are raging and out of control. *Which one is real? Did I do something to make them change? Can I do something to make them change back?* What we never seem to realize is we have no control, and can never be good enough or pleasing enough to make the alcoholic happy.

Most kids have nightmares involving monsters breaking into their homes or rooms. My worst dreams were about being trapped-unable to escape the monsters living right in my house. In my night terrors windows refused to open, doors remained nailed closed, and I could not scream. Even if I screamed no one heard me. My only chance was to quiet and hide.

Kids who grow up living with nightmarish monsters quickly learn survival skills. *No unnecessary noise, never question adults, bite your tongue, tell nobody, stay in your room, catch some sleep whenever and wherever you can, don't let anyone else in-they have no idea what might happened to them, you have no boundaries or privacy, don't complain it could be worse, there is no truth, never express emotion, and hope is a luxury you can't afford to indulge-it will just disappoint you.* If you master all these rules you just might be numb enough to survive one more day.

Ultimately I became brainwashed into "flat affect" commonly symptomatic of mental illness. I was flat-lining through life. Bad feelings were normal and good feelings treated with suspicion. Consequently, I drank to feel anything. When I drank my behavior grew outrageous and out of control. Simply, alcohol changed the way I felt, and it worked too well.

As a teen my "flat affect" became especially apparent at school. My goal at school was to get through each day without any trouble. *School trouble would just blow up worse at home.* It would likely come up in the middle of an argument between Mom and Dad. Mom would accuse Dad of ruining his kids. Then my school problems became evidence to convict Dad of bad parenting. Ultimately I found myself in the middle of an unbearable emotional tug of war.

As a result, at school, I kept my mouth shut, avoided other people, and rarely made eye contact with anyone. Homework got done at the last minute often during homeroom. I copied it if I could, and did just well enough to get by. I was clever enough and smart enough to slide by with a "B" average, and did just well enough to get into college.

During High School other kids pushed me around. I looked like a target, and I never made enough friends for anyone to care if I was bullied. I got through most days angry, and became determined to be a success. Success was my revenge. *Some day I'm gonna show them all...* Anger is an effective survival tool.

There were a few teachers who took a special liking to me, but no one took the time to notice what a mess my life was. No teacher ever inquired or expressed concern. The few teachers who liked me did talk to me and did not seem to mind my presence. They probably liked all the kids, but to me it meant more.

Almost every good moment in middle and high school had one common denominator: my only and best friend, Mitch. He behaved crazy enough to make me laugh, and together we got in just enough trouble to make school interesting while not causing misery for me at home. I never pretended with Mitch and he seemed to accept me as I was. For that I shall be forever grateful.

Drinking Buddy

We all need to matter to somebody. At a time when I felt as though I did not matter to anyone, I meant something to Mitch. I first met Mitch in the seventh grade. We lived across town from each other and went to different elementary schools. All the school district's elementary schools combined into one seventh grade middle school; Alexander Middle School. This is where Mitch and I became friends.

Mitch was "full of the devil", as Mom would often say. I was drawn to his energy and carefree attitude. At school, he seemed to be always having fun, pulling pranks, and on the verge of getting in trouble. I was terrified of trouble at school, while Mitch did not care if he was ever sent to the office. His recklessness was foreign and exciting to me.

Other kids considered me sullen or weak and generally treated me with disdain or contempt. Mitch judged people only after he was able to get to know them. He took the time to know me, and rarely treated me poorly. He was comfortable with himself. There was no "other side" to Mitch; you got all sides of him all at once.

When I met him, Mitch was tall, wide, funny, and popular with everyone-even the girls. I could not believe he wanted to be my friend. Having a "cool" friend was new, and exciting to me. I respected Mitch and he has always respected me. He was continually encouraging, challenging, and hopeful. We had many conversations about what we would do with the rest of our lives, how much fun it would be, and how we would always be together. Through Mitch, I saw a better life for myself, and he made me feel like I deserved it.

It was also through Mitch that I began to experiment with alcohol. I wanted to feel like he felt, carefree and reckless. Mitch came by this naturally while I needed alcohol to feel that way. Through alcohol, I found for brief moments, I could get the same lighthearted feeling he had. The feeling was intoxicating, and I began to drink, and act wildly out of control. We began to drink together right after seventh grade.

The summer, between seventh and eighth grade, began especially lonely for me. There were only a couple of kids my age in the neighborhood, and they seemed to be away on vacation or attending camps. Mitch lived across town, yet I did not want to ask anyone to take me to see him. Typically the answer would be an angry "no" or an aggravated "yes." It was a time in my life when I just could not take any more anger or rejection. Therefore, I avoided asking for anything-especially favors. I dreaded the disappointment of being told "no," or of being told "yes" only to not have it not come to fruition. So I became stubbornly independent, and got myself everywhere on my own.

Sometime in August, on a day when my parents were not at home, I got the inspiration to ride my bike across town to Mitch's house. It was a long ride, but I felt a little desperate. I so badly wanted Mitch to like me. After a little contemplation I decided it wouldn't be "cool" to just show up on my bike like a lost puppy. This trip needed some planning, and pinnace. Mitch was not the kind of guy where you could just show up and ask if "he could play." I had to make a bigger impression.

Hence, I went to a neighborhood store known for selling beer to underage kids. I boldly walked in; picked up the first six-pack I saw and placed it on the counter. The cashier told me what I owed and I paid it. As I began to leave, the cashier hollered "Hey kid!" I froze, terrified, I thought about just dropping the bag and running, but I was too frightened to move. Again, he barked, "Hey kid, you want your change?" I had been in such a hurry to leave I forgot to wait for my change. After jamming the change in my pocket I turned, giggled, and left. I wrapped the top part of the paper bag around the handlebars of my bike and began to peddle across town.

This was a reckless plan; somebody who knew me might see me, and ask my parents about it, if the bag broke I would smell of beer and my parent would surely smell it, I never thought to consider Mitch may not even be home. It might be our friendship did not extend outside of school. All these thoughts rattled through my head as I continued to peddle.

After about an hour of peddling through busy traffic I found Mitch's house, and stashed the beer behind a bush in the front of his porch. As I rang the bell I was convinced all this effort had been a waste of time. I was stunned when he answered the door. My friend was indeed home, and he was glad to see me. I pointed over to the bag behind the bush and he went over to investigate. "Meier you wild man!" was his response, *perfection*...

Mitch picked up the bag, and we casually walked up to the elementary school at the end of the street. We sat at the employees' picnic table, and each of us opened a warm beer. I never thought to ask any questions or consider the danger of drinking in a school parking lot. Mitch was like Superman-nothing bad ever happened when he was around. The first few sips were bitter, but things quickly sweetened. The brew began to have the desired effect on me as I became more and more carefree, loud, funny, and dangerous. When a middle-aged janitor came out, to put garbage in the dumpster, we offered him a beer. He shook his head, laughed, and walked back in the school. Recklessness was foreign to me, and quite intoxicating. For many years following, I found myself wanting that same feeling. I seemed to need alcohol more when I was with Mitch. It was the only way for me to join him in his powerful life energy. This pattern continued for years, and I never could "catch up" or "keep up" with him. Drinking just became another thing he was better at than I was.

I never cared much for alcohol, never liked the taste, and I always got incredibly sick from it. Alcohol did make me feel temporarily euphoric. I loved the exhilarating feeling it gave me, and would suffer almost anything to occasionally get it. I was unable get to this feeling while sober. Yet, alcohol was instantaneously effective as it only took one or two drinks for these feelings to arrive. Alcohol is a great liar because almost as soon as the feeling arrived it left, and no matter how much more I drank I could never get it back. If only I could have stopped when I got the initial good feeling, but I had no control over alcohol. I always went too far, and drank excessively. My entire life was out of control, and alcohol was just another part of it.

I was not in control of alcohol it was in control of me. Typically after a few more drinks, I grew angry and bitter. A few more drinks and I was helpless and uncontrollably sick. I did not consume alcohol it consumed me.

I now realize I was using alcohol to self-medicate my mental illness. I drank to feel normal, even if it was for only a flash. I wanted to feel like my friend Mitch felt, giddy and irresponsible. Now that I am under a doctor's care, and I am professionally medicated, I have little desire for alcohol. I feel normal most days, and it is indeed an intoxicating feeling.

Mitch and I remained friends for many years. We worked in the same restaurant for years, briefly attended college together, and now live near each other in the Rochester, NY area. Along the way we laughed and drank many nights away. During our single years, each of us fell in love and out of love with a variety of girls. Each of us had our own set of personal problems, and was there for to help each other through each crisis. Until I met my wife, it felt like he was the only one who had ever cared about me. At a desperate time in my life, he cared enough to reach down into the well of my despair and save me.

Mitch accepted my battles with mental illness with love, respect, and admiration. I tried to be a loyal friend as he fought some of his own demons. Neither of us drinks any longer.

In Mitch's presence, I was accepted unconditionally. Even when I was sullen or angry he did not push me away, rather he pulled me closer. I trusted him enough to share my thoughts and hopes with him. He respected me enough to listen carefully without passing judgment. The amazing thing (to me) is he always treated as though I was the best man he ever knew.

I love Mitch, and will always be grateful to him for his spirit and friendship. With deep sadness we have become estranged, and no longer communicate. We became very different people, and Mitch no longer found a need to continue our friendship. I reach out to him on occasion, and anxiously await a rekindling of our friendship.

Dead Night

I have spent much of my life obsessed with my own death. Death has been an unsettling, yet reliable companion. I cannot remember a time when visions of my own funeral have not wandered just below my consciousness. Constantly ruminating about my funeral, and imagining what people will say or think about me after I am gone. The genesis of this is often fatigue. Occasionally I fall back into old patterns and work/worry myself into total exhaustion.

During these times, I am vulnerable to my death obsession. *I'm tired of fighting-life is not meant to be so hard. I need to slow it down and rest.* Death becomes the ultimate alibi for giving into the fear and loneliness of constantly fighting my own psyche.

When I was a child, I remember thinking death would be the penultimate revenge. Everyone controlled the way I felt. I became happy, sad, in pain, lonely, or afraid based on the whims of drunken dysfunctional adults. Through death, I could finally control their feelings-make them feel pain (at my whim.) *Everyone who had hurt me would finally be hurt.* Death put me in control. The most intoxicating part of death was the liberating feeling of freedom from pain and struggle. As life went out of control, I contemplated the one thing I could control-my own death. Death was the perfect sedative.

I was too cowardly to kill myself. I blamed myself for living. I felt guilty just being alive. These feelings stay near to me. Any form of rejection puts me in the energy of my guilt for being alive. *I don't belong here-anywhere. Please, don't let them catch me...* Rejection continues to hit me like a body punch, and I have always been easily bruised. What others think of me is essentially, how I view myself. I let everyone else determine my value, and I have little sense of who I am.

I have never felt like my life was justified. I never felt "heaven sent"-never meant "everything" to anyone. Rather I have always carried an empty heart as though I was alone in the world. Rationally, I know I mean everything to my wife, son, and daughter, but it doesn't feel that way. Part of being dysfunctional is the replaying of self-defeating and false feelings: to summarize John Bradshaw, "Being in the emotion of the wounded inner-child." These frozen emotions are what keep my behaviors so child-like, and unproductive.

I need to be adored, to be reminded of how much I am loved, to be thanked, and reminded how needed I am. If not, I act hurt or rejected. Consequently, I often reject people before they can hurt me. I push people away perpetually feeding my loneliness and despair.

The alienation (I feel) creates an inner desire to prove my worth. It has never been good enough to merely fit in and get along. I need to be exceptional. I need to be the drunkest, funniest, angriest, most charismatic, most popular, saddest, best father, and best teacher anyone ever knew. Because I cannot do everything I am a perpetual disappointment to myself.

In some ways this *need to belong* has pushed me to accomplish many things I am proud of; I am a terrific teacher, a loyal friend, as well as a loving father and husband. Yet, I rarely enjoy or revel in these successes. It is a challenge for me to live in the moment. Rather I live for what I call my "one day" rewards. "One day" people will thank, appreciate, honor, and miss me after I am gone.

Those of us who grew up with alcoholism in our homes and hearts never live in the moment. The past is a nightmare we fear, and we are destined to relive our pasts for eternity. The present is full of fear, pain, and deep loneliness. We cry alone in our rooms, plan revenge, and (if we have hope) we dream of a wonderful tomorrow; tomorrows where we might live carefree, connected, safe, and loved without reservation, tomorrows where we hang on to life desperately rather than wishing it away.

There have been many times in my life when others have thought of me as courageous or optimistic. Courage is easy when you do not care if you live or die. Optimism is a necessity for survival when life is hopeless. Courage and optimism are just two of my many survival skills.

Stubbornness has been my friend for a long time. Normal people likely think of stubbornness as a negative quality, but for victims of childhood abuse it is an essential tool. The ability to focus on one thing, and to move towards it unceasingly, without needing help or advice, to ignore what everyone else says, to believe completely in what you are doing-this is stubbornness. For me it became a path to survival, even achievement.

In an abusive/dysfunctional home everyone around you is sick, emotionally, physically or both. They cannot be listened to, they do not know what is right, and may even want you to fail. All of the players are masters of self-destruction. *A child must be awfully stubborn to ignore all that, and still achieve.* Typically, the goal is mere physical or emotional survival. All of it is completely exhausting. *Any wonder a permanent rest can be so appealing?*

How can we stay alive? We need desperately to discover life is exhilarating. Doing important work and doing it well is energizing. People can be trusted, and they can help lift us when we are low. There is beauty and symmetry in the world for us to see. Simplicity and peace are safe and good-cherish these moments. Be in the moment-enjoy the struggle. All the best things are achieved through struggle. Helping others and being connected to people can lift us and enlighten us rather than exhausting us.

When we are most exhausted we need to join the human race, not leave it. Find good people, connect with them, and ask for a little help. Tell people how you're feeling-let your "true-self" out. Believe there is a higher purpose for us, and search for it.

We are sent here for a reason, and if we stay calm and patient, it will reveal itself to us. People who have been given the greatest struggles have more important lessons to learn. We may have important work to do with the strength and wisdom we earned. Our pain is not an end, but rather a beginning. Ask yourself "How can I use this journey for the common good?" "Is there somewhere I am needed?" Does God have a plan for me I have been too angry to see?

Some of the most compassionate people you will ever meet are those of us who have lived in the pain and chaos of an alcoholic home. It might be there is someone else you can help; by listening, sharing a story, or by letting them see how vulnerable you are-so they will not feel so alone. There are so many of us… How can we feel so alone?

Be quiet, alone, and at peace. Let the answers to these questions come to you. Pray for help, and for the wisdom to know why you were sent here.

Making a Scene

From the approximate ages of 8-14, I suffered from relentless bouts of fainting. As I felt faint, I grabbed at chairs or tables to steady my wobbly legs; typically I just crashed to the ground. I usually fainted in my first few steps after getting up from a chair. At the time I was convinced I suffered from a weak heart, and would die at anytime. I know now I was likely having panic attacks. I never saw a doctor about my fainting. In fact, rarely did anyone take notice of my collapses. There was only one time anyone ever reacted to my episodes, and that was when I fainted while answering the door.

My brother Ted had friend named Rick, who stopped by and knocked at the door off our kitchen. I got up from a living room chair to answer the knock, and within seconds of opening the door I had fainted-right in front of Rick. Rick became quite hysterical as my mother rushed into the kitchen to see if I was all right. By that time, I was staggering to my feet, and assuring everyone, I was fine. Mom spent the next several minutes convincing Rick my fainting was nothing to worry about. She was clearly more concerned with Rick's reaction to my fainting than with my actual fainting. Once Rick calmed down my mother's concerned ended.

In a home ravished by alcohol my mother's response seemed quite normal. My fainting was another problem to manage, and dysfunctional families have difficulty prioritizing. My health rated the same importance as poor television reception, leaky pipe, or my father's drinking. Each problem got a temporary patch with the hope they would resolve themselves.

My mother's first priority was preventing Rick from fussing, rather than dealing with my fainting. We were completely overwhelmed by the problems created by alcoholism, and incapable of responding to any new crisis.

"Keeping the lid on" is a common mantra in homes where emotional survival is the only daily goal.

My quiet nature let them assume I was doing fine. My family believed no one had to worry about me. I resembled a paid bill, filed away. Dysfunctional homes label, and categorize everyone. When a crisis hit, my family performed an emotional triage. Crises were placed into three categories: immediate emergency-minimize, too tough to fix in the long run-rationalize or deny, and lastly everything else-ignore it. While Rick's hysteria was labeled "immediate emergency" my fainting was categorized as "too tough to fix", and given lower priority. After all I seemed fine, now.

Alcoholic families compulsively worry about how everyone else perceives them. I had embarrassed the family in front of Rick, and it was the embarrassment which needed fixing-not my fainting. Therefore, I continued to faint, and no one seemed to notice. Eventually, I stopped fainting. It was at this same time I first began self-prescribing alcohol for my anxiety.

Shame evolved into my family's primary shared emotion. There was so much wrong with my family, and we were so incapable of handling any of it, we were terribly ashamed of the mess we were in. Consequently, I never let my friends into the house. No one ever stayed for dinner, and if I had sleepover, it took place in a tent in the backyard. More often I went to other kid's homes, and hoped they did not mind having me around all the time.

When my parents had their friends over to the house, it always centered on drinking. My parents were quite charming when they entertained. I looked forward to seeing their friends, and we all had fun.

Occasionally everyone would have too much to drink, and my parents would begin to argue in front of the company. Typically, their friends joined in for gut-wrenching discussions of love, sex, parenting, or careers. In the morning, the arguments were forgotten, and life continued as it had before. If I could get to sleep before everyone drank excessively, I would avoid the arguments. Most of the time I laid in bed, and listened to my parents' darkest personal secrets openly discussed. These were issues best kept between my parents, not shared with friends, and especially not shared directly or indirectly with their children. Since they never seemed to remember these fights, I think I worried more about their relationship than they did.

I lay awake worrying about divorce, violence, and infidelity while they passed out and slept. In normal homes, the parents lay awake worrying about their kids. In a home, where one or both parents are alcoholics, the kids lay awake worrying about our parents. The adults behave like children and the children behave like adults.

Dead Tired

As the child of an alcoholic I lived with overwhelming fear and deep sadness. I crept through the shadows of existence often afraid to breathe deeply for fear of losing control or falling apart. During these times my insanity led me to near total exhaustion. I went without sleep, lying in bed hyper-vigilant agitatedly waiting for chaos to terrorize me.

My mind compulsively sorted through all the horrific possibilities.

How drunk would Dad be whenever he got home?
How drunk would Mom be by the time he arrived?
Would they both be so incredibly drunk there would be no limits to their mutual cruelty?

Too often the answers to these questions were even worse than I anticipated. Living with mentally ill people (who also drink alcohol) is like starting a campfire by pouring gasoline on hot coals. There is little doubt the result will be explosive, but when will it blow and how big will it be? It's this constant uncertainty, the fear of impending violence, the random cruelty, and the possibility your life may be dramatically, permanently altered (by these insane alcoholics), which most torments a child. Questions echo through your brain as they play a psychological version of Russian roulette with their own lives as well as your own.

When Mom and Dad drank traumatic questions bounced off the walls… and I heard them all.

Had Dad been with a woman that night, as Mom had accused?

Were some of us kids from different fathers as Dad had claimed?

Did Dad really drink because he hated us all?

Did Mom drink because she hated him?

Was she really going to leave him, and would we soon live somewhere else with new friends and a new school?

Would Dad really kill her if she did?

The next day they did not even remember the awful accusations they had made, but I did…

They often drove me to complete physical and emotional exhaustion.   My gnawing desire to sleep peacefully, my desperate need to numb the sadness, my yearning to be carefree, and the daily fatigue of trying to get through each day, often made death seem alluring.   By constantly burning adrenalin my brain chemicals were permanently altered and I grew chronically depressed.   All I knew was that life was *too damn hard*, and death seemed easier.

During desperate moments I fantasized lying naked in a warm bath, my wrists open, with the blood and sadness dripping out of me-no more pain, sleep, quiet… *They would all miss me, and I would be away from all of it-safe. Finally out of the shadows and into the soothingly warm light.* The pain was locked inside, and frozen from my exterior. I never let any of it out afraid I would never stop crying and never regain control.

I cannot recall having ever wept. Skinned knees made me cry, and frustration has occasionally brought a tear to my eye, but I have never wept. Not once has all my sorrow been exposed or released through a cleansing sob. There are many nights I dream of weeping. I am being held in a faceless someone's arms as I take a deep breath and let go from a place hidden deep inside. When I awake I realize how good it felt in the dream. I try to weep, but I cannot. I am emotionally constipated.

Emotions are a slippery lot, and they tend to get their way. They leak out in a variety of cute little ways, and sometimes they get impatient with these little trickles and burst through without warning. My anger and sadness seem to be in a lifelong dysfunctional relationship. Neither one is good for the other but they are always together. They have honeymooned inside me (for a lifetime) like Alice and Ralph Kramden.

Children lived emotionless lives in our home. Any expression of emotions was met with disdain, contempt, and anger. If one of us ever expressed anger Dad's response grew outrageously disproportional and pushed our pain into the background. We learned our anger provoked such an incredible response it really was not worth it-*best to keep your mouth shut.* Additionally we would all end up dealing with Dad's reaction and likely never even acknowledge our own issues. We ate our emotions three meals a day.

When sober I tended to be guarded, withdrawn, stoic, and cold. Take a drink (even one) and I could feel all those emotions seemingly ooze out of my skin. As though I had swallowed so much poison you could smell it on my breath and skin. There was no ipecac for this poison. I had to survive it, or let it slowly kill me.

When I drank all my guardedness melted away. After just a few drinks I was (temporarily) euphoric. It felt so good to feel the release, and the euphoria. I danced all the dances, told all the jokes, and talked to all the girls.

On the other hand after a few more drinks I was bitter, cynical, sarcastic, and vial. *What happened to that ecstasy I had just a few minutes before? A few more drinks ought to put me back in the groove.* A few more drinks were always inevitable. Then I was drunk, angry, and cruel. Thinking about it now I am surprised I still have a wife and friends. If I had any doubts I had gone too far my body always insisted on telling me. I always became violently ill. Each time I drank too much I vomited and dry heaved for several hours.

A rational person might assume a victim of alcoholic abuse would logically avoid perpetuating alcohol abuse on others. A normal person would just stop drinking or never start. I was anything but normal, and the briefest of highs overshadowed any of the consequences. Those few interludes of euphoria were completely intoxicating. Euphoria for me is what most people call "normal." Just to feel like everyone else seemed like an incredible "high" to me.

Depressed people have what the psychiatrists call "flat affect." We are emotionally flat-lined. Experts would probably call it "flat-lining" if it did not sound so similar to death. Considering we are "emotionally" dead it seems more accurate than "flat affect."

I never felt playful, silly or giddy except when I drank. It's like crossing a dessert without water and you find a clear cool stream so you drink so much cold water you choke it up. The water tasted so incredibly good you could not possible consume too much of it.

Since I have successfully treated my depression I have no desire to drink. There are so many other ways to feel euphoric that alcohol almost seems common and unimaginative. Normal is fun. After the medications kicked in and leveled out I felt rested, interested, engaged, challenged, and curious.

On many occasions I talked to a co-worker about my treatment. Being as she had gone through treatment for depression, and she was a good listener. On one of the first days I experienced an elevated mood I walked up, smiled at her and said "So-this is what 'normal' feels like?" She gave me a hug, and said "Yes, you deserve it..." I remember that day as my first among the living.

I now get "high" from less destructive things like achievement, faith, family, friendship, companionship, and love. Nature leaves me aghast. I see hope in the eyes of children. I yearn to read and write the language. I have a relationship with my savior Jesus Christ. I am alive.

Bar Exam

By the time my sisters and oldest brother moved out of the house, Dad, Mom, and my brother Ted were all alcoholics. I was left alone living with three alcoholics. The next four years became the most difficult of my life. It was during this time I attended college. While I attended, Ted mostly worked and drank; Dad spent his off hours at taverns, and Mom sat at home drinking away her loneliness.

Each night Mom entertained herself with beer and television. After dinner most nights Mom walked down (she never learned to drive) to the corner store and bought herself a six-pack. Sometime during this period, the six-pack became an eight-pack.

On a typical night Dad arrived at home-drunk, spoiling for the fight, and Mom was ready to oblige. I believe Mom wanted Dad to find her drunk just to see what she had been living with for so many years. Of course, these two angry drunks always got the loud violent fight they wanted. Ted typically arrived long after both of my parents were tired of fighting. Usually drunk, he tried to sneak off to bed as quietly as he could-just to avoid any hassle. Some nights Dad was still looking for a fight, and he waited at the kitchen table for Ted to come home.

My brother was an angry young man, and could not resist my Dad's baiting. These arguments became some of the most violent. Dad always knew just the right comment to set Ted off on a tirade. It was only a game to Dad. I think he wanted to prove he was a better drunk than Ted was. As their argument got more heated, Mom typically staggered out of her room to Ted's defense. Three raging alcoholics smashing around the kitchen made for an "interesting" study environment as I tried to prepare for classes the next day.

Many late nights, I spent cowering in my room trying to write a paper for school. I hoped they had forgotten I was around, and left me alone. On occasion one of them dragged me into their fight to confirm or deny some point they wanted to make. The whole situation was pointless because I was the only one who ever remembered what they argued about. If they did remember, they were too sick the next day to discuss it.

Living with these three alcoholics, it was nearly impossible to succeed in college. In addition to my schoolwork, I was also working as a bartender and waiter a few nights a week to pay the tuition. Some nights I did not leave work until 4am. This incredible chaos resulted in exhaustion, anger, and the beginnings of my own more serious problems with alcohol.

I cannot imagine a more demented job for me to have than as a bartender. Serving drinks was not the most disturbing part; rather it was the availability of free drinks for the bartender. Part of my job was to "prime the pump" and get people drinking by drinking with them. Drinking with them put more money in the cash register, as well as in the tip jar. When drinking I took on an outrageous and playful persona behind the bar. I worked closely with another bartender, and we had a lot of gimmicks to get the tips flowing; practical jokes, drinking games, and throwing bottles back and forth. This newfound confidence and popularity was enticing.

The worst of my drinking occurred during my bartending years. I was never able to have just a couple of drinks. I always wanted too many, and it almost ruined my life. Was I an alcoholic?   I do not know and I no longer care about the answer. I have forgiven myself and live now without alcohol in my life. I am also convinced I can never use alcohol safely, and I can never have a normal relationship with alcohol.   Whether alcoholism is learned behavior or genetic I will leave to the scientists, I just know I cannot drink-ever.

I made it through college with a "B' average. How I did so well is still a bit of a mystery to me. I know I worked hard, but I still do not fully understand what drove me to work quite so hard. The usual answer to people give to a question like that is "determination." *Anger* might be the most accurate description for the driving force behind my success in college. For me college was not to be enjoyed rather it was to be conquered. It was the enemy, and I was going to win.

Surviving my college years is one of my proudest accomplishments. I have always felt alone with it. I never wanted a family celebration, or party. It felt like I had survived a plane crash. *What was there to celebrate?* My struggles were my own and only I alone had earned the victory.

Spirits

I yearned for a childhood home filled with love and peace, but I never had one. So I wanted a loving home even more for my own children. Creating a loving home became one way of defeating my own childhood fears and loneliness. Similarly, fatherhood gave me a chance to prove I was not like my own father. Indeed, I am not my father. The home I created is warm and loving where childhood is nurtured, and affection is shared by all. I adore my children and they me.

There are times when I get incredibly sad watching their carefree demeanor. I am jealous of them as well as a bit resentful. *What would I have been like if I had even a little bit of the love and support they have?* My imagination wanders into many wonderful scenarios. *I could have been a lawyer, politician; I could have led people to do great things...* I am learning to spend less time wondering what I could have been and more time appreciating how far I have come.

I believe the challenges I grew up with have meaning and purpose. I once heard author Gary Zucav explain it this way (paraphrasing) ... "You were given the parents you needed to have. In order to learn the lessons you needed to learn. So you can do what you were sent here to do." As a father, from a wounded childhood, I may understand my children's emotional needs better than some parents. I have lived without love, and I can still feel the pain. I know I am a better teacher because I made it through the suffering and struggles of living in a home torn by alcoholism. I am a better man having survived it all.

It is difficult to take wisdom from these struggles, but I continue to learn, mostly from children. They are my best teachers. They are certainly my most unguarded and honest teachers.

There are many times when a challenging student will enter my life and push me to complete frustration. At those times, I look deep inside them to see their fear, anger, and sadness. I know it's there for I carried those same feelings with me. Because I know their pain so intimately I typically respond with empathy and love-rather than anger. I know the profound impact a loving teacher has on a child for a wonderful teacher cared enough to love me.

Scientists have discovered that dolphins can sense when a disabled or injured swimmer is placed in the water with them. Amazingly the dolphins seem to recognize a swimmer with a mental or emotional handicap. Upon gaining this insight dolphins become more engaging, affectionate, increasingly gentle, and keenly helpful.

Children seem to have a similar sensibility. Many students approach me concerning emotional issues. They need help or they just need someone to listen to them. Often they tell me they *sensed* I would understand and I could be trusted. It's as if, like the dolphins, they sense my injury and find me more approachable. I believe adults (too often) put out a blanket of invincibility and perfection, which intimidates many children. On the other hand, if adults became more openly vulnerable children might approach them and share intimate pieces of them. I believe this is why lectures from adults do not work. A lecture implies the lecturer has overwhelming expertise, and this can act as a belittling force field blocking meaningful dialog.

I attended sixth-grade at Pine-Hill Elementary School, where Mr. Schuler taught Social Studies. He was tall, well dressed, respected by his colleagues, and loved by his students. He emanated calmness and strength. I wanted desperately for him to like me, and he did. Mr. Schuler found my sadness to be thoughtful, my outbursts an expression of enthusiasm, and he told me I had character and courage. Mr. Schuler saw things in me I did not even see in myself. He made all his students feel that way, and not one of us ever doubted he meant it. I trusted him. If I did not know an answer he taught it to me, and if I did not understand, he showed me. He helped me have hopes and dreams of what *could* be.

Many of my teachers were mere taskmasters, evaluators, or disciplinarians, but Mr. Schuler was a "teacher." I learned a great deal of World History from him, but more importantly, I learned what a teacher could be, and what a man should be. The year I spent with him in sixth grade gave me the passion to become a teacher. I wanted to make kids feel (about themselves) the way Mr. Schuler made me feel about myself.

I spent the last twenty seven years trying to live up to the example Mr. Schuler set for me. The moments I am most proud of are the times when I see a trace of hope on a face where there was none before. The idea I may be able to help put a little light into some child's world makes the memories of all the sadness and pain bearable.

There are a thousand books about how to teach, but I have found there are two essential components of teaching; kids have to know you genuinely like them, and you have to help them be successful-everything else is mere accessories. The lesson plans, curriculum, technology, organizational skills are nice, but kids can learn without them. Without love and success, no amount of paperwork is going to help.

When people talk about the great teachers, or the life altering school experiences they had, curricula or lesson plans are never mentioned. What people say about great teachers is... "They saw something in me I did not see." or those teachers made them feel good about themselves. These people changed their own view of the world and their futures.

You can train "good" teachers, providing they work very hard, but no training can make a "great" teacher. These rare few, like Mr. Schuler, were sent here with a spirit, which lets them love the unlovable and inspire the uninspired. Mr. Schuler was sent to me, and he made all the difference.

N.A.

Drinking was an integral part of my life. I became known at work as a "guy who worked hard and played harder." I earned this reputation socializing with co-workers, and behaving outrageously after I had a few drinks. After a few beers I became the "life of the party", and ran around like my hair was on fire. In truth, I was mentally ill and alcohol removed all restraints on my personality. When I drank people saw the uncensored, full screen version of my insanity.

When a psychiatrist diagnosed me with post-traumatic stress disorder, obsessive-compulsive disorder and bi-polar disorder I stopped drinking permanently. To stop self-medicating with alcohol frightened me, but mental illness frightened me more so I decided to give psychoactive drugs a chance.

With a little "buzz" (from alcohol) my anxiety melted away. I loved feeling relaxed and normal. So I drank, danced, sang, hugged, and laughed with abandon. After a few more drinks, I behaved badly, and in the end, I often drove home drunk. Upon arriving home I argued with my wife, and felt very much like my father's son. The knowledge of my mental illness empowered me to stop. I had enough reason to never start drinking. At first socializing with friends (who drank) was hard, but it got easier. Now I enjoy not worrying about hurting somebody's feelings, being caught by the police, killing someone while driving, or vomiting. I cherish my sobriety.

My transition to sanity had many challenges. Because I stopped being manic, people wondered, "What happened to you?" "Relax, Loosen up..." or "You used to be so much fun." They counted on me for their entertainment, and I was letting them down. I informed all my friends I was taking prescription medication, and I was forbidden from drinking alcohol-I left out the mental illness part.

When the medications gained effectiveness, sobriety became easy. I discovered feeling normal ended any desire for alcohol. I no longer needed to alter the way I felt, because I felt good/normal most of the time. Living with mental health became challenging, interesting, controllable, and even fun. I am perfectly capable of drinking occasionally, but I choose not to. Mostly to remind myself how insignificant drinking is to me.

Friends eventually supported my sobriety. They seem to enjoy my calmer good nature, and rarely ask me to liven up a party. My friendships are deeper and more satisfying. People respect and trust me. I am a better listener, more empathetic, patient, and I tell them how I feel about them. They never have to wonder if I'm speaking from an alcohol-induced euphoria. People always get to speak to my authentic self.

Additionally, I resolve conflict without taking it as a personal attack. I am not so easily hurt, and therefore less hurtful of others. My wife no longer has to be afraid of agitating me, and starting an argument. We have fallen in love all over again. This time we have fallen in love as two healthy individuals who desire each other, rather than needing each other. Mental health was a hard fought victory, and I earned it.

Sobriety allows me to truthfully tell my students I do not drink, and that I still have a good time. I want my own children to feel the joy and pride of my sobriety, and to let it shape their relationship with alcohol. Sobriety is an integral part of who I am. Now it is clearer to me how many problems alcohol create in so many lives. Society excuses and justifies drinking in a variety of ways. Some parents think as long as their kids are drinking and not drugging they are doing a good job parenting. "Just drinking" is now acceptable even preferred behavior. In fact, much research indicates nicotine and alcohol are the two biggest drug problems in America. High School students tell me they try to have "alcohol free" graduation parties, but their parents insist on the presence of alcohol. Many parents believe a party with alcohol served to minors is acceptable as long as they take away their car keys. Have we emphasized not driving drunk so much so that *drinking* has become completely normalized for minors? We give away condoms in schools to promote safe sex maybe we should provide limousine service to kids so they can get home from parties safely.

It seems to me the message we are sending our children is that alcohol is an essential and irresistible part of life. I now know alcohol is an unnecessary part of life, and I only regret it took so many bad experiences for me to learn.

The Road Home

Recovering Adult Children of Alcoholics live with profound sadness. They obsessively long for a new story-dream of a new story-the life that should have been. This dream is full of simple moments, full of dinners where faces are lit with anticipation, and voices chime in with silly nothings. They dream of places where parents converse with in intimate whispers and a parent's hand runs through their child's hair just to let them know they are loved. They yearn for a home where warm baths are followed by sweet smelling pajamas, and children fall asleep smiling. They yearn for a life where little friends play at *your* house, and adults keep their promises. They dream of parents who provide an endless supply of hugs, guiltless encouragement, and days looked forward to with joyful memories of gentle days, compassion, empathy, wisdom, and the random "I love you."

Adult children of alcoholics are dreamers. They wish and hope for a world unknown. They understand intimately children need to be loved for no reason at all, and need to feel as unique as a snowflake.

Many times ACOA become healers of other people's souls, and are some of the best nurses, counselors, and teachers. These soulful spirits walk among our children in hospitals and classrooms-consciously trying to give other people's children the sanity and compassion lacking in their own childhoods. Their way of creating a new story is through helping others. A life full of kindness and hope plays out in front of their eyes, and of their own doing.

Often ACOA attempt recovery but are left tainted with deep sadness, regret, wistful emptiness, and unworthiness. *Why did no one care about me the way I care about everyone else? It's not hard to do. I would have settled for so much less than I give away. What would I be like today if someone had cared for me so completely?* Some Adult Children of Alcoholics never get past their laments. Their lives are journeys toward an end they'll never find. Other times they find a road home, and live in peace and wholeness.

How do we find the road home? I am not a doctor or psychiatrist. I can only describe the road I took. These are the principles I learned from my own journey to recovery.

1. Fight for your own peace.
2. Try to understand those who have hurt us.
3. Be prepared to forgive.
4. Ask for help.
5. Explore your spirituality.

Fight for your own peace.

Sometimes we have to reach the bottom of our despair, and become completely exhausted to start fighting for our lives. Other times, we are just sick of being in pain.

I had suffered for four years with terrific sinus headaches until a wonderful Ear Nose and Throat Specialist named Dr. James Hadley convinced me he could help. After extensive sinus surgery, I was headache free for first time in years. I had convinced myself my headaches were the source of my unhappiness. *Of course I am depressed, irritable, sad, lonely, and angry-I am in constant pain.* When the physical pain was alleviated, I discovered I was still in terrific pain-emotional pain. My head was healed, but my heart still ached. My experience with Dr. Hadley taught me there were people out there to help me.

At the time, I had a poor family doctor who consistently left me feeling rather foolish for coming to the doctor, and I dreaded calling him. His lack of empathy delayed my referral to Dr. Hadley. So I finally transferred to a new family doctor, and asked him for a mental health evaluation. My new doctor referred me to psychiatrist, Dr. Joseph Messina. Through working with Dr. Messina, I learned how to be happy, and I learned I deserved it.

Try to understand those who have hurt us.

As early as I can remember, I caricatured my father into a diabolical brute whose selfishness drove him to unbridled cruelty. I feared and avoided him-even eye contact could provoke an argument. The entire house changed when he came home. Just the sound of his car sent me scurrying off to bed.

I conjure up Mom as a hero who would gladly battle Dad to protect us. The only time we had any peace was when Dad passed-out on the couch. Then we all tiptoed around so as not wake him. It was like an old vampire movie where everyone was gathered around the vampire hoping to drive a stake through his heart before he awakes. Suddenly the sun sets, and as the hero is about to strike the hammer to the butt of the stake... as vampire sits up.

As kids we all longed for isolation, whether it was having a television in our bedroom (we had a couple of them over the years-they worked if the antennae was set just right), or our own playroom in the basement, the goal was solitude. We all wanted a safe place where we could avoid the "ogre" and his arguments with my mother that was certain to come. My child-like simplifications of Mom and Dad lasted well into adulthood.

Neither of my parents were the caricatures I had imagined them to be. Dad was a highly wounded man who had his own dark corners and demons to run from. He had a story just as I did. Dad had a brutal manipulative father, and a smothering mother. They were left homeless by the machinations of trusted a relative. Dad suffered from asthma and watched friends go off to war while he was labeled unfit for service. Dad anesthetized his demons by drinking. None of it excused his cruelty, but it did put a question in my mind. *Had he done the best he knew how?* "Maybe" was enough of an answer to pry a crumb of forgiveness from my hardened heart. He was a complicated man who had pain and regrets just as I did. *Would I really have done better than he, if I had walked his road and traveled his journey?*

Mom was not the heroine I had portrayed her to be. It was clear in the letter we found after my father's death. Some part of her liked battling and caring for my father. She had lonely empty spaces, and needed my father's frailty. Mom battled Dad, yet she never had the strength to protect us from him-often she provoked him, and later became an alcoholic as well. I know much less about my mother's story. I do know she felt ignored by a cold father, and never felt worthy of decent treatment.

These two dysfunctional people gave me just enough love and support to convince me life was worth living. They took me on a very difficult journey, and it has made me a better man, and a better father. I may not have gotten the parents I wanted, but (possibly) I got the parents I needed.

We cannot hope to understand or forgive ourselves until we understand those who have afflicted us with so much pain. Their story is our story.

Be prepared to forgive.

Understanding is not the same as forgiving. Understanding is principally an intellectual pursuit while forgiveness is a spiritual journey. Forgiveness is a slow winding river fed by the tributaries of love, hope, and faith. Only when this river is gorged with water can we flow to the sea of peace.

We need to love ourselves enough to believe we deserve peace.

We need to love those who hurt us enough to give them the gift of peace.

We must love life enough to want to spend it free of anger and bitterness.

We must believe there is a joyful existence waiting for us.

We must understand, through forgiveness, our pain will ease.

We must hope for the strength not to pass our pain on to our children.

We need faith that (though it may be hidden from us) our journey has a purpose.

We need to recognize everyone (even those who hurt us) as a child of god.

Finally, we need enough faith to let go of our pain.

I learned how to forgive my father when I wrote and delivered his eulogy. A friend who had managed to forgive his own father recommended psalm 148 (included in it's entirety in the back of this publication) to me. It praises God for the heavens, the sun and moon, the trees, and even the mountains. Conversely, Psalm 148 thanks God for the sea monsters, the storms, along with fire and hail. The conclusion of Psalm 148 reminds us we all are creations of God. We may not appreciate the storms in our life, but they are necessary and they are perfect creations of God. *Who are we to resent their role in our lives?*

I included Psalm 148 in my father's eulogy, and I neither denied nor condemned his flaws. Rather I professed publicly that God sent him to teach me many things, and ultimately I was a better man for it. I had forgiven him, and it was too late for him to try to dismiss it or give it back. He was going to rest-forgiven.

Ask for help.

After living in (self-imposed) emotional isolation, the thought of asking for help was daunting. I prided myself on doing "it" alone whatever "it" was. I thought of my emotional scars as battle wounds symbolic of my manhood. I distrusted people-they were unreliable, and I believed no one would help me. *I might get a few spare moments of their time, but not much more.* I refused to ask for help, I visualized only inadequate and frustrating responses. People close to me disappointed me, and I had come to expect it of everyone. ACOA often learn to have low expectations of people, it insulates us from the inevitable disillusionment of being let down.

While some children grow up thinking they are the most important things in their parent's lives, ACOA believe they are annoying burdens who ought to feel lucky for any scraps of attention thrown their way. We are the "crumb-snatchers" of love eternally hoping some scrap of attention is left behind for us. The thought of injecting ourselves into another person's life (with are own needs) is foreign to us. *They have problems much more important than mine.* We are experts at minimizing our emotional needs. We gnaw at our problems like a tough piece of meat. We swallow problems whole, and they stick in our throats to choke us.

There is terrific vulnerability in asking for help. For me the most intense fear I had was someone minimizing my pain, and making me feel silly or weak for not coping better. Much of the pain I experienced was ignored or denied so I lost all instinctual knowledge of what was normal, bad, difficult, outrageous, or abusive. I learned to be a "black and white" thinker with poor judgment of "shades of gray."

I approached my recovery with trepidation. Since I was the only person, I completely trusted, I decided to confide in myself first. I wrote down a couple of my experiences and tried to read them with an omnipotent eye. I wondered if my experiences really were as bad as they felt. After careful reflection, I gave some of these works to my wife to read. I expected the usual grammar corrections and a maybe a hug.

Remarkably, Andrea wept for me. No one had ever loved me enough to weep for me. She left me a note the next day telling me how sad she was I had suffered so intensely. This validated my desire for help, and I finally possessed the courage to ask for it.

Being an undiagnosed obsessive-compulsive, I arrived at my family doctor's office with a typed list of my anxieties and compulsions. I was urgently referred to Psychiatrist Dr. Joseph Messina's for an evaluation. Through the compassion and wisdom of Dr. Messina, I was able to begin the long journey of reclaiming my life.

People are often reliable, compassionate, even loving, and some of the best of them will give a great deal of their time and energy to others in need. We merely need to have the courage or desperation to ask. When we find these people, we need to nurture the relationship and keep them close to us.

Explore your spirituality.

What holds this work together, and initiates the healing is a sense of purposefulness. *It all happened for a reason.* There is healing energy in believing a higher power chose this path for us as part of a greater plan. We yearn to find the reason for the heartache. What are we supposed to understand (about ourselves or the world) through the arduous journey we continue? *What are these people sent to teach us, and have I learned it yet?*

I believe all suffering has a purpose, and the greater the suffering the higher the purpose. I have often heard parents of challenged children describe them as a gift from God. My perception for years was this was just a way of putting a positive spin on a terrible tragedy, and those parents needed to believe such things to get through the day. I now understand this is not at all what these parents mean. Rather, their special children taught them to be more loving, compassionate, and empathetic. They have learned to become the people they were *meant* to be.

My suffering was intentional, and through my growing belief God is continually revealing his intentions for me. From it, I have learned how to love and forgive. Through it, I have become a better father, husband, and teacher.

My belief in God and the exploration of my faith is mine and mine alone. None of us takes the same journey. For many of us spiritual exploration is the most intimidating part of healing, the "deal breaker" of wellness. It may help to think of spiritual exploration as a walk through the woods in search of our base camp. We each take our own path through the woods. Some of us get lost for a long time, and some of us find our true path right away. Some of us meet obstacles and danger while others of us do not. Yet, at the center is the same warm fire with welcoming friends happy to take us in to cheer us and feed us. There is a place for all of us. There is purpose in our journey. We can all come to the same place with our own stories to share.

The Mourning After

Danny

I had died-murdered by alcohol and insanity. So much of my life was wasted buried alive in sadness and guilt. Then again, was I ever alive?

There was a time when life was carefree and simple. I can see it in pictures of myself-up until about age seven. The boy in the picture had a devilish smirk and seemed full of life, showing a prized fish caught at Bob's Lake-playing the guitar I got for my first communion, or posing with my pals from pee wee bowling. I had the look of a typical little boy, excited, curious, and even childlike.

In later photographs, it is as if an eclipse had blocked out all the light inside of me. Looking at those pictures I see a forced half smile, shyness, moody, loneliness, boyhood left behind. Somewhere between those two sets of photographs I died.

It seems I have spent my entire lifetime mourning my own death. I see my siblings as witnesses to my own execution-fearful that they will remind me (even joke) of the murder. Imagine going through life constantly reliving your own murder. Seeing the murderer and the witnesses constantly, and no one else seems to miss you or even notice you are gone. Inside they are dead too, and mourn the loss of what they could have or should have been. Together we form a tragic dysfunctional dance of ghosts-the undead. Unaware we no longer exist. I am now aware of my own passing-the passing of little boy named Danny. R.I.P. Danny.

Danny was a good boy, funny, imaginative, popular, loving, playful, and cute, even adorable. He had many friends, and dreamed sweet dreams, dreams of being awakened to another sunny day, as if every day was the first day of summer. Everyone was glad to see him, and he was glad to see every new day. Danny stared out the window during naptime, wandered the neighborhood on great adventures, and had to be dragged home at dusk. I miss him so much. I almost forgot what he looked like, and yet I have just begun to mourn his loss.

Somewhere around age seven or eight Danny died suddenly. That carefree little boy stopped wandering the streets, and the devilish grin faded. He was replaced by a moody, sullen little boy who preferred his own company to that of his buddies. His face became full of loneliness and shadows. He was frightened all the time, and he responded guardedly, even to his closest pals.

I miss the lovable Danny. I see parts of him in my own children. Sometimes I find myself jealous of my own children's carefree spirit. It has been a lifetime since I felt that way. I have to let that sad little boy go, and become something new. Danny will never return it has been too long, but I have carried the loss far too long.

If I let go of the grief who or what will become of me? What is inside me waiting to be released? Who am I? I may spend the rest of my life finding out. Now that I have begun grieving, I feel ready to begin to know myself again.

Dad

My father was old and sick before I could stop hating him. I learned to accept my father for who he was without mourning who he was not. This was challenging, but I did it and it led us both to an acceptable level of forgiveness.

Dad's long illness and eventual death exposed the complete dysfunction of our relationship. After years of smoking, Dad had finally quit, but the damage was irreversible. He knew he would spend the rest of his life gasping for breath until his lungs could no longer take oxygen from the air, then pass away gasping for his life. This scenario terrified him and he thought about it constantly. On occasion he would look at us teary-eyed and mumble "What am I gonna do?' There was no answer. We knew the progression of his disease. His self-pity constantly reminded me how tired I was of being the adult in our relationship. I recall with sadness and regret that I did not have enough compassion left in my heart for him.

During his final years, when I should have cared for him, I felt as though I had (we all had) already done a lifetime worth of care giving. I had nothing left for him. My life was a mess, and I was barely making it through each day. I was lonely, depressed, and anxious every minute of every day. It was obvious to everyone close to me I was in trouble. Yet, my Dad never noticed or inquired about how I was doing. It never occurred to him I might have my own problems… I might need my father.

My father only worried about himself as he always had and mumbled pathetically "What am I gonna do?" I had no answers. Dad was going to die, and he was going to do so in an increasingly ugly way. He had done so little on his own, throughout his life; it was unreasonable for me to expect he would be able to die with dignity. Cruelly I did not intend to help him die. This one thing he was going to have to do on his own. Maybe he sensed it and it truly terrified him… he felt alone.

Dad was not alone my sister Missy largely tended to his every need and carried the burden, as my mother would have if she were alive. I think Missy was trying to work out her own relationship with Dad as he slowly died, but it seemed to elude her. Dad showed her no mercy or gratitude. I admired her strength and wished I had it.

Forgiveness

My father suffered for five years before he died of emphysema. Years of smoking and drinking had finally destroyed his body. During these last years, he used oxygen continually and had limited mobility. Dad lived alone in a safe, clean apartment building overlooking Main Street in a wealthy Buffalo suburb. My father was capable of taking care of his daily needs at home, but leaving his apartment was trying for him.

My sister Missy developed a strategy, which allowed all his children to share the burden of his care. The four children who lived (in the area) agreed to each alternate spending several hours one Saturday each month, caring for him. Minimally this involved laundering his clothes and grocery shopping, typically it became much more.

My father had become a terribly frightened man. I came to understand he likely had always been a frightened man, and he used anger to release the fear and alcohol to sedate it. Now as he edged toward death his fear was overt. He needed his family. Yet he knew we did not have much good will left for him. Sadly, he was unwilling to acknowledge the pain he had caused, and therefore little healing could take place. Like his body, the damage was done.

Instead of trying to heal his relationship with each of us, he continually tried manipulation, and guilt to get what he needed from his children. Each of his five children coped with his manipulation quite differently. Carol lived in New Jersey and tried to handle many of his economic and financial issues. She drove many hours a few times a year to see him. Missy cared for Dad with incredible love and patience, often sacrificing her own life and happiness. Marty became increasingly intolerant, and had many contentious visits. Eventually he stopped coming or only stayed briefly.

During this time Marty's marriage failed and my father's situation, certainly exacerbated Marty's suffering. Remarkably, Ted hit bottom, went into recovery, and had a personal renaissance. He fell in love, got married, and fought his way to sobriety. Ted and my father inflicted terrific pain on each other over the years. Yet, Ted found the courage and compassion to forgive him, and became a very generous son.

My own relationship with my father had many set backs, and disappointments. I became increasingly mentally ill, suffering from depression, and obsessive-compulsive disorder. Consequently, I was particularly unforgiving of Dad's manipulative personality and completely intolerant of his frailty. I was increasingly unable to ignore the many years of disappointment and anger I had with my father. These visits were often ugly as I failed him and myself on many occasions.

During my typical Saturday visit; I made every attempt to keep busy moving around the apartment cleaning or leaving the apartment to run errands. I watched the clock until it appeared reasonable to leave, and then rather abruptly I left. If I stopped and visited with him he would become distraught and hopeless about his illness in an attempt to gain my sympathy for few minutes longer. This was what he understood of love: pity was the deepest expression of love to him. In the beginning of my monthly visits I was too angry with him to pity him, and too depressed to help him out of his own depression. Mostly, I was intolerant of him, and we parted in anger.

Almost as soon as I arrived back home, he called me on the telephone to try to fix everything we had said in anger. My wife called it the "follow-up phone call." My role was to reassure him I was not "really" angry, and the ill words were a mere misunderstanding. Typically I lied and told him I was not angry with him, he always seemed relieved. This pattern continued for almost two years.

After about two years of contentious visits, my sister Carol gave me some insight and advice that changed some of my (and Dad's) sick patterns. Thankfully, I was in therapy and becoming strong enough to listen to her. Carol explained Dad felt as though I was looking for an excuse to leave as soon as I walked in the door to see him. It was true; I hoped I had disguised it better. Furthermore Dad was incredibly lonely, and looked forward to my visits more than he let on.

Therefore, he tried to manipulate me into staying longer than I intended. If it took pity, or guilt to keep me there a while longer, then so be it. Her advice was to put aside the whole day, and to act as though I had the whole day to spend with him. Hopefully the visits would become more pleasant, and it would not seem like such a burden. *You might even start to look forward to going...* she said.

I was usually too stubborn to take advice, but I was ready to listen. Our visits improved immediately. He was even willing to leave the house, and go out for a hot dog or ice cream. Dad seemed to always know where to get a good hot dog for lunch. Many times I brought my children along with me and they got to know their grandpa a little better. We certainly never became best friends, but occasionally we were able to talk about baseball or current events. In the last year of his life we spoke frankly and had heated exchanges about the past. These were real conversations where I spoke my mind and he listened. The outcome of this was a more adult relationship between us.

We began to end each visit by telling each other we loved each other, and at my Dad's insistence... we hugged. For the briefest of time I felt like I had a father and he felt like he had a son. When Dad died, we both held sweet memories of these visits. I think if he had been sober, during my childhood, we would have been friends.

My deepest regret is it took so many years for me to become strong enough to work out my relationship with him. Many people say "A tough life makes you stronger." If this were true then children from alcoholic homes would be Supermen. Instead, I grew fragile and sad. Living as a child of an alcoholic made me incredibly weak and vulnerable.

My father was a very unhappy man. The reasons he was so unhappy I will never really know. It may have been his childhood; my grandfather died before I was born, and we rarely talked about him. Therefore, I know little of my grandfather. Although those who did know him often tell me, my father turned out pretty good "considering." It might be Dad suffered his own brand of hell on earth. I know now, because of stress and/or genetics, he likely lacked certain brain chemicals. Regardless he had an incredible hole inside of himself he could never fill. He tried to fill it with cigarettes, anger, sleep, work, and most of all alcohol, but it never worked for long. His neediness and weakness was his way of asking for help, and I resented him for it. *Why couldn't he love me enough to stop drinking? Why was he so unhappy? What happened that made him so disappointed in me?*

His illness lives on in each member of our family. We carry it as sure and directly as if it were a birth defect. We are each left alone with the burden of his anger and sadness. The demons of his heart no longer torture my Dad. For those of us who survived, we must try to understand, forgive him (and ourselves), care for each other, learn to love, and most of all we must do better for our own children.

For all of us who are victims of an alcoholic there is hope. Through some combination of sharing stories, group work, psychotherapy, faith in god, love of friends and family, and through medication, we can reclaim our lives. We have the power to make the pain stop. Victims are around every corner and in every neighborhood and they need to hear your story as much as they need to tell their own. If reading this book provokes dialog on the subject then it has been a huge personal success. Thank you for letting me share my story with you.

Forgiveness

Psalm 148

1. Praise the LORD!
   Praise the LORD from the heavens;
   praise Him in the heights!
2. Praise Him, all his angles;
   praise Him, all His hosts!
3. Praise Him, sun and moon,
   praise Him, all you shining stars!
4. Praise Him, you highest heavens,
   and you waters above the heavens!
5. Let them praise the name of the LORD!
   for He commanded and they were created.
6. And He established them forever and ever;
   He gave a decree, and it shall not pass away.
7. Praise the LORD from the earth,
   you great sea creatures and all deeps,
8. fire and hail, snow and mist,
   stormy wind fulfilling His word!
9. Mountains and all hills,
   fruit trees and all cedars!
10. Beasts and all livestock,
    creeping things and flying birds!
11. Kings of the earth and all the peoples,
    princes and all rulers of the earth!
12. Young men and maidens together,
    old men and children!
13. Let them praise the name of the LORD,
    for His name alone is exalted;
    His majesty is above earth and heaven.
14. He has raised up a horn for His people,
    praise for all His saints,
    for all the people of Israel who are near to Him.
    Praise the LORD!

Acknowledgements:

Many thanks to my siblings-we survived. Hank Paszko for helping me let Jesus Christ into my life. To Ed Mathews for the appropriate kick in the butt. Love and thanks to Andrea, Lorelei, and Garrett.